# Teachers, Change Your Bait!

## Brain-Compatible Differentiated Instruction

## Martha Kaufeldt

Crown House Publishing Ltd.
www.crownhouse.co.uk

*Teachers, Change Your Bait!* is a text grounded in the realities of classroom life. It is a thorough yet digestible mix of brain research, learning theory, and psychological principles with specific strategies and activities that enhance teachers' ability to differentiate teaching and learning in their classrooms. Particularly noteworthy is how each chapter concludes with Tackle Box Ideas, which summarize the guiding principles that open each chapter. Martha's relatable "teacher-down-the-hall" style drew me into a conversation about learning that both validated and challenged my educational beliefs and practices. This book, in its entirety or by individual chapters, would make an excellent professional development focus on differentiation. Bravo, Martha, for placing a truly valuable tool in the hands of educators!

—Mark Reardon, coauthor of *Strategies for Great Teaching*,
the HotTips series, and *Quantum Teaching*

What a joy to find a book that provides essential information in such a warm and engaging manner. Martha has a sense of humor and she uses it to convey her passion to make sure the learning style of every child is understood and respected through brain-compatible learning. Martha gets it right when she says, "If you want 'no child left behind,' then use various strategies to bring all children along." This is a must-read for everyone who cares about children and education.

—Jane Nelsen, Ed.D., author and coauthor of the Positive Discipline series

Martha has tackled one of the most important topics in education. Using her brain-research expertise, she provides a process that will hook all teachers—both novice and veteran. Read this book and you'll be convinced that differentiation is a philosophy you can embrace—hook, line, and sinker!

—Marilee Sprenger, author of *How to Teach So Students Remember*
and *Becoming a "Wiz" at Brain-Based Teaching*

I am so excited about Martha's new book! It skillfully provides practical applications for differentiated instruction and step-by-step guides to help beginning as well as experienced teachers provide a safe, secure, and productive learning environment for *all students.*

Teacher Down the Hall stories let the reader know that the ideas presented are doable and do produce effective results. Modeling; lecture; discovery learning; inquiry method . . . there's something for everyone. And there are even ways to work with parents . . . what a bonus!

Martha talks about lessons being "meaningful, relevant, and worthwhile." I would use these same adjectives to describe the book. There's enough research to cover the theory aspect, but it's the hands-on activities that make the book a wonderful resource in any teacher's hands.

—Dr. John Abbott, director, Teacher Preparation and
Certification Program, Region VII ESC, Kilgore, Texas

Martha Kaufeldt is brilliant at helping teachers teach better! The information she shares about brain research is presented in such an easy, effective way, and her years of practical classroom experience make her an instant mentor to both seasoned and rookie teachers alike. *Teachers, Change Your Bait!* will change your life, and ultimately the lives of your students.

—Charla Belinski, certified parent instructor, International Network for
Children and Families, and board member, Aspen Youth Center

I am extremely grateful to Martha for her willingness to share her considerable wisdom, and I admire her skill in creating a book that is fun and easy to use. Following her guidance has made a world of difference in my classroom. Teachers will appreciate the wealth of practical ideas, and they will watch with joy as their students respond to a brain-compatible environment.

—Shane Sparks, intermediate teacher, Tierra Pacific Charter School, Santa Cruz, California

*Teachers, Change Your Bait!* is the best [book on differentiation] I've seen. It has the right amount of theory; based, as it should be, on how the brain learns best. It is organized and written in teacher-friendly language and balanced with anecdotes. I like the way Martha distinguishes between low-prep and high-prep strategies so teachers can feel it is possible to start small and work toward more differentiation as they became more skilled. I am excited about using this new book myself and sharing it with others so we have Martha as our own "teacher down the hall."

—Sue Nieland, third-grade teacher, Bangor Elementary School, Bangor, Wisconsin

Martha Kaufeldt, in her new book, has continued to capture practical and timely strategies that teachers can use tomorrow to make a difference for children in the classrooms all across North America. The book is a skillful blend of the latest brain research, sprinkled with real classroom anecdotes from over twenty years of teaching, humorously translated into examples to which all educators can relate.

Teachers and educators will find many useful hints and examples of relevant applications of brain-compatible strategies along with lesson ideas that teachers could reproduce and adapt for classroom use tomorrow.

—Ainsley B. Rose, director of education-curriculum, Western Quebec School Board

Martha Kaufeldt has done it again! *Teachers, Change Your Bait!* is an invaluable, user-friendly book that takes you step-by-step through exactly how to set up and implement a brain-friendly, differentiated classroom. Her explanation of the key elements of brain-compatible, differentiated instruction, and the practical suggestions for doing it, are the best I have read anywhere.

Martha calls herself "the teacher down the hall"—a teacher who is always doing strange and interesting things to make sure everyone "gets it." In addition to the hundreds of practical, easy-to-use teaching/learning strategies, the book is sprinkled with stories about "the teacher down the hall" gleaned from her years in the classroom. These stories are in and of themselves worth the price of the book.

In the current climate of increased testing and accountability, as the way to supposedly improve our schools, *Teachers, Change Your Bait!* is a breath of fresh air. I heartily recommend this book to any teacher who is serious about leaving no child behind!

—David Lazear, President, David Lazear Group, Inc., best-selling author, consultant, and trainer in *applied* multiple intelligence

Teachers faced with ever-expanding demands to meet standards and the needs of diverse populations will find this book a virtual treasure trove of ideas that are practical, well illustrated, and most importantly, brain compatible. In a few words, "Grab this book!" You'll be forever grateful to Martha Kaufeldt for writing it.

—Pat Wolfe, Ed.D., author of *Brain Matters* and coauthor of *Building the Reading Brain, PreK-3*

First published by
Crown House Publishing Ltd.
Crown Buildings, Bancyfelin, Carmarthen, Wales, SA33 5ND, UK
www.crownhouse.co.uk
and
Crown House Publishing Company LLC
4 Berkeley Street, 1st Floor, Norwalk, CT 06850, USA
www.CHPUS.com

Editing: Melanie Mallon
Design, typesetting, and cover: Dan Miedaner
Illustrations: Julia van der Wyk
Illustrations on pages 98 and 136: Greg Burros
Author photo: Carola Nettles
Clipart: All clipart courtesy of Clipart.com, per membership terms and conditions

ISBN: 1904424619

LCCN: 2004111442

Printed in the United States of America

# Contents

Contents

# Acknowledgments

One might think that for someone as verbal-linguistic as I am, the writing process would come easily. It doesn't. I avoid and procrastinate, often choosing to do laundry or organize the canned-food cupboard instead—tasks that provide immediate feedback and satisfaction. I am always motivated to make presentations and share the content and ideas with groups, but being tethered to the computer for hours to capture it on paper seems tedious. I need a gentle taskmaster who provides skillful nudges and frequent feedback. After the publication of *Begin with the Brain* in 1999, I felt excited about and proud of the final product. My patient editor, Veronica Durie, cheerfully said, "So when can we expect the next book?" Very funny.

I have been a slippery client, always on the run and living a full family life. I have been more involved in *learning* than in teaching. As a mom to Kurt and Kris and stepmom to Greg, I have discovered that no matter how much you think you know about teenagers and parenting, it is a tough job, and you must continue to differentiate your strategies with each child. With my dad, I have learned about the mysteries of Parkinson's disease and the miracle of newly developed procedures such as DBS (deep brain stimulation; see http://www.mayoclinic.org/movementdisorders/deepbrain.html). After two incredible surgeries to implant electrodes in his brain, my father is able to drive and continue participating in life. With my mom, I have learned about patience and the incredible antibiotic-resistant "superbugs" that have evolved. After reconstructive back surgeries, she developed a life-threatening staph infection that is classed as MRSA (methicillin-resistant *Staphylococcus aureus*; see http://www.cdc.gov/ncidod/hip/Aresist/ca_mrsa_public.htm). After a difficult year of physical rehabilitation and *daily* IV antibiotics, she has begun to show signs of recovery. And from my dedicated and loving partner of four years, Rick, I have learned that there are huge differences between the male and female brains. But he has also taught me to make sure to schedule in time for *play*, something I often forget or neglect to do.

I dedicate this book to my editor and friend Ronnie Durie. Her perseverance, loving kindness, encouragement, and gentle nudging have finally come to fruition. I love the product but struggle with the process. She connected me with editor extraordinaire Melanie Mallon, who streamlined the editing process and made me feel like a writer. Ronnie kept me going—more than any editor would, could, or should. Her friendship means a lot to me. Thank you, Ronnie. You are a *keeper*!

# Beginning with the Brain

In the early 1980s, I had an opportunity to begin my study of brain research and its implications for teaching and learning. For almost two decades I have been putting research into practice at all grade levels. I have been able to use the fundamental concepts of brain-compatible learning as the keystone to understand why almost every innovation and educational trend either succeeds or ultimately fails. Those strategies and programs that are well grounded in what the human brain needs to be successful usually survive.

I happen to be fascinated with the ever-expanding field of cognitive neuroscience. I am compelled to keep up on recent research and discoveries. My family calls me a "brainiac." In my work as a consultant and workshop presenter, I have found that teachers most frequently ask questions such as "Can you give me just the basic concepts of all this?" "What can I do first?" "Can you give me a jump start?" In our profession, we are used to getting the basic ideas, and then innovating and elaborating on our own over time.

With that in mind, it makes sense to focus this series about successful teaching and learning strategies on brain research. *Teachers, Change Your Bait! Brain-Compatible Differentiated Instruction* is the first in a continuing series I will be writing called Beginning with the Brain. Subsequent titles will focus on topics such as brain-compatible classroom management and assessment strategies, all rooted in differentiation.

## The Teacher down the Hall

For many years and in several different schools, I have loved being "the teacher down the hall." I enjoy sharing ideas, innovations, brainstorms, and struggles with anyone who would like to listen. As a mentor and coach in several comprehensive staff-development programs, I have had many opportunities to be a friend and helper for various colleagues. I know how overwhelming it can be to be a good teacher. There is never enough time, and there is always something else to be done. The educational pendulum swings, and we hang on for dear life. Having a friend down the hall to get ideas from is a good thing, I think.

Like the other books in this series, this book is designed to be some words of wisdom and summary from your teacher friend down the hall, as if I had gone to a workshop or summer institute and now were sharing the information with you. I call this the Name That Tune method: I share the key concepts with you in brief forms that are recognizable (that is, not just fragments), along with Teacher down the Hall Stories in which I share my own experiences with these concepts and brain-compatible learning in the classroom. By summarizing this incredible information, however, I don't want to trivialize it. I have included resource suggestions in the Tackle Box Ideas section at the end of each chapter and in the bibliography (page 173) in hope that you will be inspired to investigate further.

## Here's a *TIP*! Theory into Practice

*Brain-research based, brain friendly, brain-compatible learning, or brain-antagonistic?!* The idea of designing classroom practices, strategies, and even schools on specific findings from neuroscience may seem a bit reckless and a giant leap to some skeptics. I have found, however, that even small revelations from brain research may be translated by clever teachers into classroom strategies that elicit huge results for many students. I refrain from using the term "brain-based" when describing the learning theories I embrace. If the brain is the organ for learning, then wouldn't all teaching strategies be brain-based? Making statements such as "Brain research proves . . ." doesn't work either, because the research alone doesn't prove *anything*. What I do believe is that valuable information is discovered every day about our brains and minds. I encourage teachers to learn as much as they can about current understandings and research. As a responsible educator, I am committed to designing curriculum, strategies, and environments that are most *compatible* with what we currently understand about how our brains function and learn.

The growing field of *cognitive neuroscience* will continue to provide answers to questions about both the biology of the brain and the influence it has on our behaviors and thoughts. Neuroscientists at prestigious universities are conducting fascinating studies on how brains grow, solve problems, remember, deteriorate, change, pay attention, and influence behavior. Unfortunately, there are two main drawbacks to the usability of the recent brain research: The types of studies being conducted demand that the variables be carefully controlled; thus, using animal subjects is the norm. Incredible findings are determined from observing rat, primate, and even sea-slug brains. Conducting what is referred to as *translational research,* behavioral studies are then arranged, and eventually, usually years later, the initial theory is interpreted and suggestions for application are disseminated. *Whew!* I don't think my students can wait that long.

Aside from this delay in putting research into practice with human brains, there are important areas in neuroscience that must take priority. Studies regarding the causes and effects of devastating diseases such as Alzheimer's, Parkinson's, epilepsy, multiple sclerosis, schizophrenia, and depression are essential, and answers must be found soon.

Consequently, neuroscientists don't have many suggestions ready for classroom teachers on how an average brain (if there is such a thing!) might best learn and remember information. "One small step for man, one giant leap for mankind." those famous words of Neil Armstrong as he walked on the moon reflect my philosophy about using recent brain research to *influence* everyday classroom practice. I believe that well-informed educators can take a small step from brain research and create and apply a reasonable strategy in the classroom that will help many students take a giant leap in their learning.

With all the findings from research about how our brains react to stress, lack of stimulation, poor nutrition, lack of physical activity, and emotional or traumatic experiences, one can more easily determine what things can *diminish* proper brain function. I have found that in my classrooms, I am mostly trying to create a learning environment that at the very least is *not brain-antagonistic.* I don't want the abilities of my students' brains to be minimized—I want them *maximized!* Perhaps it should be referred to as *brain-friendly* education.

We can't wait for the neuroscientists to tell us what to do with our classes of unique learners. Knowledge about our brains is growing exponentially. Brain biology can offer some new directions and inspiration to educators. We must continue to read and discuss the findings and do our own action research in our classrooms. This is what I have been doing for over twenty years. I can assure you that building your teaching around strategies that are most *compatible* with how the brain learns will be a rewarding experience for your students and for you.

Interested in the latest cognitive neuroscience studies? Keep an eye on these researchers and their work. Several have written books that you will find fascinating:

Harry Chugani, M.D., Department of Neurology, Wayne State University;

Antonio Damasio, M.D. Ph.D., Department of Neurology, University of Iowa;

Daniel C. Dennett, Ph.D., Center for Cognitive Studies, Tufts University;

Michael Gazzaniga, Ph.D., Center for Cognitive Neurocience, Dartmouth College;

Barbara K. Given, Ph.D., Adolescent Learning Research Center, Krasnow Institute and Graduate School of Education, George Mason University;

Alison Gopnik, Ph.D., Department of Psychology, UC Berkeley;

Patricia Goldman-Rakic, Ph.D., Department of Neurobiology, Yale University;

William T. Greenough, Ph.D., University of Illinois, Urbana-Champaign;

Eric Kandel, M.D., Howard Hughes Medical Institute;

Kenneth Kosik, M.D., Harvard Medical School;

Joseph Le Doux, Ph.D., New York University;

Helen Neville, Ph.D., Psychology Department, University of Oregon;

Robert Sapolsky, Ph.D., Neuroendocrinologist, Stanford University;

Arnold Scheibel, M.D., Professor of Neurobiology and Psychiatry, UCLA Medical Center;

Daniel J. Siegel, M.D., Center for Culture, Brain, and Development, UCLA;

Larry R. Squire, Ph.D., UC San Diego;

Paula Tallal, Ph.D., Center for Molecular and Behavioral Neuroscience, Rutgers University, Scientific Learning Corporation;

Stuart M. Zola, Ph.D., Department of Psychiatry and Neurosciences, UC San Diego School of Medicine;

and James Zull, Ph.D. Professor of Biochemistry, Case Western University.

# Introduction

## *Common Sense to Common Practice*

Good teachers have always known that one size doesn't fit all, and yet they are often pressured into using instructional strategies that cover a narrow range of their students' abilities, interests, and readiness levels. This *teach to the middle* approach neglects the capable students' enthusiasm and frustrates those with learning difficulties and special needs. Incredible educators continue on their own to develop varied strategies and techniques and will tell you that this approach is just common sense if your goal is to reach all students in your class. If you want "no child left behind," then use various strategies to bring all children along. In addition to helping all students learn the basics, educators must also use techniques to challenge and inspire our most gifted learners. Providing enrichment opportunities and expanding the core concepts also require the ability to use several diverse strategies.

Differentiated instructional strategies are what good teachers have used in common practice on a daily basis. These educators have a range of techniques they apply as needed. An exceptional teacher is an innovator as well, one who continuously adapts to student needs and situations.

Differentiated instruction isn't limited to remedial strategies that help struggling students understand basic concepts and acquire basic skills. When a teacher incorporates differentiated instructional strategies, students at all levels are challenged. The bar is raised for even the gifted and high-potential students. As Carol Ann Tomlinson, a recognized author and expert in the field of educational differentiation, points out, "Differentiated instruction is first and foremost good instruction. Many current understandings about learning provide strong support for classrooms that recognize, honor, and cultivate individuality" (Tomlinson 1999, 18).

**DIFFERENTIATED INSTRUCTION**

*Differentiated instruction* is defined by the Association of Supervision and Curriculum Development (ASCD) as "a form of instruction that seeks to maximize each student's growth by meeting each student where she is and helping the student to progress. In practice, it involves offering several different learning experiences in response to students' varied needs. Learning activities and materials may be varied by difficulty to challenge students at different readiness levels, by topic in response to students' interests, and by students' preferred ways of learning or expressing themselves" (ASCD 2005).

## Change Your Bait

A fishing analogy fits the key concepts of differentiation perfectly. My son Kris has taught me almost everything I know about fishing. He developed this passion when he was eighteen months old, fishing off his grandparents' dock on Lake Tulloch. He developed his skills from dawn to dusk, often refusing to do other lake activities for the chance to catch another fish. He refined his skills by watching fishing shows on Saturday mornings in lieu of cartoons or videos.

The basic strategies of a good angler include thorough preparation:

- ◆ Check the weather and decide on the optimum time of day for success.
- ◆ Consider geographic location and potential fish-gathering spots.
- ◆ Recall past successes—what has worked best before?
- ◆ Know the type of fish you want to catch—what are its habits?
- ◆ Include many diverse lures and bait in your tackle box—be prepared!

- Ask other anglers who have been out recently—where have they been successful?
- Schedule enough time in case you need to keep at it for a while.

After considering all the factors, anglers select the lure or bait they believe will give them the greatest chance of catching the fish they desire, although luck will still be a factor. If after an hour, one's success or luck is waning, a good angler will *change the bait* (or the location, time of day, or another factor). Getting ready to teach a concept or skill to a mixed-ability class of students could be approached in the same way.

The basic strategies of a good teacher also include thorough preparation:

- Orchestrate the optimum time of year and day to introduce the concept or skill so that students will get it.
- Consider the best teaching location to enhance learning.
- Pull out your best resources and successful implementation strategies.
- Stock your tackle box of strategies with diverse lures.
- Discover as much as possible about the students—read files and collect data.
- Consult with other teachers about what has worked best with their students.
- Allow for enough uninterrupted time for the learning to take place.

Even though we know that one size does not fit all, it makes sense to start the instruction and learning with our best lure and see how many kids bite the first time. Use common sense to know when to reel in and change the bait or location. Differentiated instruction is simply a teacher preparing a tackle box with a wide range of teaching and learning strategies and developing experience about when to implement them. Stocking your tackle box with only one or two lures—such as the textbook program and a strategy that used to work ten years ago—will not help you hook your students. This book is designed to help you fill your tackle box with multiple strategies so that you have options as you attempt to leave no child behind as well as challenge your high-potential students.

## Align with Standards

Learning standards should drive the curriculum design. These standards provide descriptions and expectations of what all students should know and be able to do. Just as there is more than one way to catch a fish, however, there are a vast number of methods and processes to help students master the standards. Differentiated instruction as part of the learning process honors each student's unique abilities, experiences, and learning preferences while helping all students meet standards.

Each lesson design should begin with the standards to be taught. Instruction should begin with the *best guess* strategy for the particular group of students. Differentiated instructional techniques are implemented in the lesson design to expand and enrich understanding as well as to remediate or to clarify concepts that are challenging for the learner, as Tomlinson describes: "In a differentiated classroom, the teacher proactively plans and carries out varied approaches to content, process, and product in anticipation of and response to student differences in readiness, interest, and learning needs" (Tomlinson 2001, 7).

Following is a list of the most common ways teachers differentiate. Each is explored further in subsequent chapters. Baby steps to begin with are outlined in chapter 11. *Remember: Implementing innovative instructional strategies may not have the desired outcomes if the learning environment isn't compatible with how the brain learns most efficiently and effectively.* Chapter 1 reviews the basics of brain-compatible learning. Use this as your foundation for success in the classroom.

## Elements of the Learning Process That Can Be Differentiated

### *Physical Environment*

- ◆ Consider the effects of environmental stimuli on the students' brains and bodies.

- ◆ Modify seating arrangements within the classroom to accommodate students' preferences.

- Investigate and use alternative work areas outside the classroom.

### Social Environment

- Establish a sense of belonging and inclusion by creating base *tribes*.

- Pre-arrange various partnerships and small groups to save time and reduce stress.

- Identify *learning clubs* as needed to reteach or to cluster students based on interest.

### Presentation

- Use novelty and humor to engage the students' attention.

- Link the new concept or skill to the here and now and to students' daily lives.

- Orchestrate a discovery process using a project, an experiment, and technology resources.

### Content

- Emphasize meaningful, relevant, and worthwhile content to motivate and challenge students.

- Engage students by teaching specific areas in depth rather than broad general concepts.

- Adjust the curriculum to match and accommodate students' readiness levels.

### Process

- Include diverse reflection activities to build long-term retention.

- Orchestrate frequent opportunities for choice using various intelligences and systems.

- Use available technology resources to gather information and integrate student understanding.

### *Products*

- ◆ Orchestrate meaningful culminating projects for students to apply their understanding through authentic achievements.

- ◆ Build higher-level tasks, inquiries, and activities using Bloom's taxonomy.

- ◆ Design diverse products and performances for students to demonstrate their understanding.

The best instructional strategies, however, will not provide the intended results if implemented in a brain-antagonistic environment. Think of differentiated instruction as an essential element of brain-compatible learning. When stating the goals for differentiation, keep the brain in mind. The more we know about this wonderful organ for learning, the more we will be able to design environments and curriculum that match how learning takes place naturally and efficiently—for each unique learner.

**BRAIN-COMPATIBLE DIFFERENTIATED INSTRUCTION**

Teachers differentiate by orchestrating powerful learning experiences in response to every student's unique needs, guided by brain-compatible teaching and learning concepts:
- creating a safe and secure climate and environment
- designing meaningful and engaging experiences, tasks, and activities
- using flexible grouping and collaboration
- providing immediate feedback and ongoing assessment
- allowing adequate time for active processing
- orchestrating opportunities for individual choice within an organized system

# 1
# Begin with the Brain
## *Key Elements of Brain-Compatible Learning*

▶ Maintain a safe and secure climate and environment to maximize the brain's capabilities.

▶ Provide multisensory experiences in enriched environments to stimulate brain development.

▶ Orchestrate multiple opportunities to reflect on and actively process new knowledge.

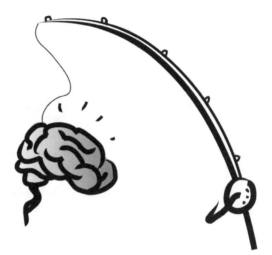

*R*ecent dramatic advances in our understanding of the human brain and cognition ensure that the cognitive neurosciences will play an increasingly important role in educational policy and practice during the 21st century. (Sylwester 2005, xv)

In the last couple of decades, many educators have begun to rethink the structures of schools and the way in which curriculum is designed and implemented. The emerging research findings on how the human brain learns and remembers are beginning to influence decisions about discipline, social structures, classroom experiences, physical movement and comfort, nutrition, student stress, and lesson content. These findings have led to brain-based, or brain-compatible, learning, in which the emphasis is on the learning process. Many of the researchers' recommendations are what good teachers have always done intuitively. In the ongoing effort to leave no child behind, more teachers realize the need to understand the fundamentals of the learning process and improve teaching practices based on how the brain learns best.

**BRAIN-BASED TEACHING**

"Approaches to schooling that educators believe are in accord with recent research on the brain and human learning. Advocates say the human brain is constantly searching for meaning and seeking patterns and connections. Authentic learning situations increase the brain's ability to make connections and retain new information. A relaxed, nonthreatening environment that reduces students' fear of failure is considered by some to enhance learning. Research also documents brain plasticity, which is the brain's ability to grow and adapt in response to external stimuli."

—ASCD (2005)

The brain research collected over the last decade as it pertains to learning and memory can be summarized for educators into the three main categories listed at the beginning of this chapter. Understanding these elements and using them as the foundation for everything we create and plan in our classrooms can help us create schools that are more closely aligned with how the brain learns most efficiently and effectively. In addition to these three, many additional areas can and should be explored to help us understand learning disabilities, extended stress, emotional disorders, and physical handicaps.

## Maintain a Safe and Secure Climate and Environment

*The classroom climate and environment must be conducive to learning. A classroom that is physically uncomfortable or maintains a threatening atmosphere or tone will minimize students' brains' ability to function at their highest potential. Understanding some of the latest research about how our brain reacts to stress and fear can help teachers know what not to do and begin to know what to do.* (Kaufeldt 1999, 2)

A brain-compatible classroom maintains a safe and secure climate and environment to inhibit perceived threat and helplessness. When learners feel threatened, intimidated, excluded, confused, incompetent, or physically unsafe, their brains respond reflexively and shift into survival (fight or flight) mode. The fight-or-flight response causes an overproduction of noradrenaline, which in turn causes the brain to focus on survival rather than on learning and actively processing new information (Kaufeldt 1999). Eric Jensen summarizes the brain's reaction to stress in this way: "The brain wants to make sure that when the negative stress is strong, creativity is set aside in favor of the faster easy-to-implement rote, tried-and-true behaviors which may help you survive. As a result, under moderate to strong stress or threat, you'll get very constricted, predictable behaviors" (1997, 23).

Whether a reflexive response occurs due to a perceived threat or to an exposure to true danger, when reacting, most human brains are less capable of doing any of the following:

- being creative
- seeing or hearing environmental clues
- remembering and accessing prior learning
- engaging in complex tasks, open-ended thinking, and questioning
- sorting and filtering out unimportant data
- planning and mentally rehearsing
- detecting patterns
- communicating effectively

## Teacher down the Hall Story

Many years ago, I had a student in my fifth-grade class who was absent often and usually unprepared when she did show up. Hannah (not her real name) was quiet and frustrated that she was behind in her work and was always having to play catch-up. When I investigated what the problem was, I found out that she was the oldest sibling in a household with several children and a single mom who was a full-time university student. A stressful life I'm sure.

Midway through the year, after a nasty custody battle, Hannah's father abruptly took her away to another state. I never heard from her again and always wondered whether the new home and family had been a good thing for Hannah.

A few years ago, at a workshop I was doing, a young teacher approached me and said, "Mrs. K, I'm Hannah." I started to cry and hugged her and asked about how things had turned out for her. As we talked, there was one thing she said that will stay in my heart forever: "You know, I'm embarrassed to say that I don't really remember *anything* specific that I learned in your class that year. But I will always remember one thing. No matter how many days I had been absent, or how late I was that day, or how unprepared I was, your class *always* made me feel safe, relaxed, and cared for." She said that she could count on the security and the consistency that my class provided even when things were rough at home.

This is a perfect example of how a brain-compatible classroom environment can really be a safe haven for students who are at risk and under extreme stress for any reason.

Clearly, the reflexive response minimizes the brain's capabilities, and therefore, helping kids (and their brains) feel safe and secure has to be our first and foremost goal if we want to maximize learning. In each of us, as unique individuals, the reflexive response is triggered by different stimuli and degrees of pressure. This delicate balance of what is too much stress and threat and what is appropriate challenge and pressure is imperative for teachers to know about each student.

Common school situations that cause the reflexive response in most students include

- fear of potential physical harm
- embarrassment, humiliation, put-downs
- inadequate time to complete a task or to reflect
- not knowing what's going to happen next
- challenging work with little available help or support
- chaos, confusion, lack of order
- isolation or not feeling a sense of belonging and inclusion
- emphasis on competition and extrinsic rewards
- activities that appear irrelevant or have an unknown purpose

In the last decade, neuroscientists have explained that even as this survival response is happening, the sensory information is traveling to the cerebral cortex for a more rational evaluation: "If this more thoughtful reflection suggests that we have overreacted, the brain may send out a message to counteract the reflexive message" (Kaufeldt 1999, 4). This reflection on the situation takes more processing time. Our prior experiences and previous exposures to situations may help influence our ability to make a decision and an action plan and begin to act thoughtfully. When the stress has been resolved, the perceived threat is removed, or the reflection suggests that we no longer need the survival mode, the brain releases the appropriate hormones to counteract the adrenal surge.

> Even as we defensively react to stress or threat, we size up the situation and create a plan. The brain shifts from reaction to action.
>
> —Martha Kaufeldt (1999, 6)

Creating a safe and secure physical, emotional, and social environment must be our first step in maximizing learning for *all* of our students. (Chapters 3 and 4 provide more specific detail about creating this environment.)

## Provide Multisensory Experiences in Enriched Environments

Research on what is referred to as *brain plasticity* grew exponentially in the 1990s. Neuroscientists such as Dr. Marian Diamond and others have concluded that although most of our 50 to 100 billion neurons are present at birth, they continually grow, develop, and make connections throughout our lifetime (Diamond and Hopson 1998). When the learner has multisensory experiences in enriched environments, some neurons are prompted to grow *dendrites*—small branches that make connections with other neurons to create new neural networks. "The brain goes through physical and chemical changes when it stores new information as the result of learning" (Sousa 2001, 79).

Dendrites become strengthened the more frequently the *synapses* (neural connections) are stimulated. Memories are formed when a group of neurons are activated and fire together. Without frequent stimulation, the brain may prune those branches that aren't being used. The saying "use it or lose it" seems to be true of the brain's connections.

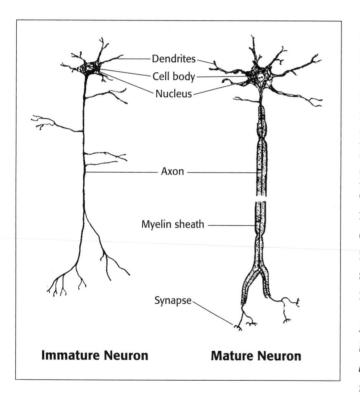

**Immature Neuron**     **Mature Neuron**

Meaningful experiences can change the brain's structure, size, and density. The brain responds best when the learner sees meaningfulness and can make a connection to prior experiences. If the task is too difficult, developmentally inappropriate, irrelevant, or not challenging enough, the brain is not inclined to engage. The necessary brain chemicals are not released, dendritic growth is not stimulated, and optimal learning does not occur.

*More than any other organ, the brain can be shaped by stimulation and use. . . . The dendrites, the magic trees of the cerebral cortex, retain their ability to grow and branch, and it is this lifetime growing potential that enables us to continue learning and adapting. However, childhood is a particularly crucial time for the brain because of neural sculpting that goes on; for many of our abilities, tendencies, talents, and reactions, those that get "hardwired" in childhood become the collective mental platform upon which we stand and grow for the rest of our lives.* (Diamond and Hopson 1998, 56–57)

The best instructional strategies could prove futile if the content of the curriculum is not meaningful to the learner or lacks coherence. The brain is constantly scanning for stimulation. Strong emotional connections also increase the chance of the brain engaging. In his book *How the Brain Learns*, David Sousa states that to increase the chance that a student will remember the lesson, a teacher must address two questions: "Does this make sense?" and "Does this have meaning?" (2001, 46)

In *Making Connections* (1994), Renate Nummela Caine and Geoffrey Caine introduced twelve brain-mind principles. These principles have been expanded more recently in their book *Mindshifts* (1999). Many of these principles emphasize the importance of relevancy, connectedness, interactive complex experiences, emotions, and attitude:

*The search for meaning (making sense of our experiences) and the consequential need to act on our environment is automatic. The search for meaning is survival oriented and basic to the human brain. . . . The search for meaning cannot be stopped, only channeled and focused. . . . Provision must be made to satisfy our curiosity and hunger for novelty, discovery, and challenge. Lessons need to be generally exciting and meaningful and offer students an abundance of choices.* (1994, 89)

Two main issues for educators emerge from the understanding of brain plasticity:

1. In the United States, we are in an era of standards-based curriculum and high-stakes testing. Classroom time has been focused on proficiency, performance, and test-taking skills, and seatwork and repetition have become the norm. Discovery time, creativity, play, physical movement, visual and performing arts, projects, field trips, simulations, and so forth are being reduced to "nonessentials." Without these valuable experiences and opportunities, which enrich the learning environment,

students may respond well on tests, but they will not gain practical application of the concepts being taught. Their brains won't be wired to understand the concepts, and they will lack the ability to apply those concepts to future learning.

2. Kids and families are different today. Our students are coming to us with far fewer prior experiences that might help them understand concepts taught in school. Their brains aren't prewired with some basic understandings about their world, and this may keep them from being able to connect new learning to prior concepts. For kids today, outdoor discovery play is often replaced by sedentary indoor activities. Social activity with neighborhood friends is replaced by more isolated technology-dependent activities.

Students come to us without some important wiring in their brains developed enough to attach new ideas. Teachers feel unable to help students develop new brain connections through experiential learning because educators are often instructed to focus on having kids do well on the tests. This dilemma isn't necessarily the fault of politics, parents, or economics, but might be seen as a result of our environment and of technological evolution.

Another key stage in a child's ability to understand is when the frontal lobes of the brain kick into gear at the onset of puberty. Technically, this is when the last area of the brain is being myelinated. *Myelin* is a fatty substance that the brain builds around the single axon of each neuron. This insulation promotes faster and more efficient transfer of information and messages between the neurons. Prior to this, the key "executive" area of the brain may not be fully functioning, and the ability to understand cause and effect, abstractions, time, and implications develops with maturity. As teenagers' brains develop, they have a greater capacity to hypothesize, deduct, analyze, think logically, look into the past, and investigate the future.

When first getting to know our students, we may make incorrect assumptions about their brains' prior knowledge and readiness levels. Now it is more important than ever before to orchestrate projects and experiential learning opportunities. These activities, which were usually expected to be done outside of the classroom, and enrichment activities that are often the first to be cut from classrooms, may be the keys to successful learning.

## Orchestrate Multiple Opportunities to Reflect on and Actively Process New Knowledge

Research also shows that after experiences in an enriched environment have prompted brain growth, "an organism's interactions with its surroundings fine-tune connections" (Society for Neuroscience 2002, 11). Opportunities for collaboration, reflection, and active processing are key to filing new information into long-term memory.

Experience may trigger brain growth and development, but the connections are not hardwired until the learner has had multiple opportunities to process the information. Re-stimulating the initial connections ensures that the learner will retain the information for the long term. There are three main ways that teachers can create opportunities for learners to investigate and make sense of experiences:

1. **Reflection**—Processing new information in various ways will help the brain store the concept in long-term memory and make it more accessible in the future. Journal writing, discussion with a process partner or group, illustration, graphic organizers, Mind Mapping, teaching someone else, and review within 24 hours all help solidify information.

2. **Collaboration**—Putting the new concept into language and having discussions with others will continue the reflection process by expanding learners' understanding as they observe and reflect on how others are

interpreting the new information. We are social beings! Some of us need to talk it out. Others may prefer to reflect on their own and gain greater understanding after hearing others' opinions.

3. **Choices**—Reflecting on and processing new information in only one way could limit learners' comprehension. If the activity isn't presented in the way in which a person learns best, such as in a student's learning style or multiple intelligence strength, then the student may not fully grasp the new idea. Having a few choices among ways to reflect and process encourages students to participate and engage in the learning process more fully.

The brain is the main organ for learning. Brain-compatible teaching is the art of understanding some brain basics and using the information to orchestrate the most effective, efficient, and engaging lessons possible. Beginning with the physical environment, emotional climate, and social dynamics, you can create a safe and secure setting where students feel comfortable, open to new ideas, and ready to learn. By emphasizing real-world projects, hands-on experiences, and meaningful tasks, you can actually prompt students' brains to grow and develop. To ensure that the learning is grasped and retained, provide multiple opportunities for students to actively process the new concepts. Strategies for developing all these ideas are included in the following chapters.

## *Tackle Box Ideas*

♦ Teach kids about their brains. Explain the reflexive response. Have students brainstorm times when they have felt helpless, confused, scared, stressed, and so forth.

♦ Build into each lesson more opportunities for firsthand experiences. Don't assume that all students have the prerequisite knowledge for a new concept.

♦ Orchestrate opportunities for reflection and processing of new ideas rather than accepting a modest level of understanding and then moving on to the next concept.

# 2
# Developing Student Profiles

## *Aligning Instruction with Individual Needs*

▶ Purposefully gather and organize data to create individual student learning profiles.

▶ Determine each student's multiple intelligence strengths, learning styles, prior knowledge, and interests.

▶ Identify developmental stages, readiness, challenge areas, and limitations.

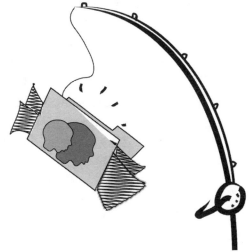

*I*f students aren't learning from the way that we teach, then we need to teach them in the way that they learn. This statement embodies the essence of ... instructional intelligence, a significant component of which is the practice of differentiating instruction. ... A dynamic concept, instructional intelligence challenges the "one size fits all" way of thinking. There is no magic program or one best way of teaching, because there is no one standard student profile. All students are different, and we need different strategies for different learners. (Forsten, Grant, and Hollas 2002, vii)

Each learner is as unique as a fingerprint. Born with a genetic predisposition and physical capabilities, each child has experiences that shape the brain into a learning machine, with its own special way of interpreting and processing the world. In addition to cognitive abilities, each of us also develops what I refer to as an *emotional threshold.* Based on our personalities, our sensitivities, and the stress factors in our lives, we develop a limit to how much pressure, chaos, and ambiguity we can handle without going into the reflexive response.

In my classroom, when I used a firm look and stern voice to tell a student, "Go sit down and get started—right now," one student might get upset and later tell her mom that I had yelled at her "in front of the *whole* class!" On the other hand, given the same directive, another student would giggle or do a Jim Carrey face and say, "OK, whatever you say! You're the boss!" It didn't faze him in the least. This emotional threshold is present, and different, in all of us. What pushes one student's buttons isn't even an issue for someone else. There do seem to be some gender differences, and there are certainly cultural influences.

If we get to know our students, we begin to understand their emotional and challenge thresholds. We have a better sense of how hard we can push and when to back off a little, and how big and how many steps we can give them at a time without overwhelming them. One of the most straightforward ways to do this is to create individual profiles of our students and add to them throughout the year.

## Gather and Organize Student Data

To begin to differentiate strategies, attempt to know more about your individual students. Creating a student profile for each student can be a great way to gather data that might influence how you address the learning needs of that student later. In elementary and self-contained classrooms, the profile can be a file folder including various surveys and instruments that provide you with a range of information:

- standardized test score summary
- reading inventory
- math skills and concepts inventory
- writing samples
- multiple intelligences checklist
- All about Me student survey
- parent/home survey and language survey
- individualized education plan (IEP)

In secondary and single-subject classrooms, each student in each class period could have a file that might include the following:

- multiple intelligences checklist
- writing sample
- career and college survey
- All about Me student survey
- individualized education plan (IEP)

An All about Me student survey can be adapted for older or younger students. (See the sample questions below.) I ask these survey questions because I want to know right away what daily

**ALL ABOUT ME SAMPLE STUDENT SURVEY QUESTIONS**

- What do you like to do best outside of school?
- What is your favorite subject at school?
- What do you do if you get mad?
- What time to you go to sleep at night?
- What commitments do you have after school? Work? Sports?
- How do you get money?
- Whom do you live with the most?
- Where's the farthest you have ever traveled?
- What do you have for a typical breakfast?
- What responsibilities do you have at home?
- How early do you get up on a school day?
- When are you most successful at school?
- What frustrates you most?
- How do you get to and from school?
- How much time a day do you spend watching TV, playing video games, and using the computer?

*Reel Good Idea*

life is like for each student. I don't want to find out casually after several months that a particular student has been having to stay one night at Dad's and then one night at Mom's, or has to take care of younger siblings while Mom works, and so on. These are all pieces of a huge, complex puzzle of influences on our students' lives. All these issues contribute to how successful a student might be on any given day.

## Determine Each Student's Multiple Intelligences, Learning Styles, Prior Knowledge, and Interests

Gathering information about your students' different intelligences, learning styles, prior knowledge, and interests will help you to anticipate each student's emotional and cognitive thresholds in the classroom. Various surveys and instruments are available for determining each student's intelligence strengths and preferred learning style.

### Multiple Intelligences

As described by Howard Gardner, a leading researcher at Harvard on the understanding of multiple intelligences (MI), an *intelligence* is the ability to solve problems or create meaningful products in a particular setting. Gardner and his team have identified at least eight ways in which we learn and know about reality that are common to all cultures, and he believes there may be more. Each of us has unique strengths based on our genetics and environment. Each person is "smart" in his or her own way. By discovering and building on those strengths, we can help students use their intelligences to enhance their understanding of new concepts. The eight intelligences Gardner identified are the most common or preferred processing and problem-solving abilities:

- ▶ verbal-linguistic: "word smart"
- ▶ logical-mathematical: "logic smart"
- ▶ visual-spatial: "picture smart"

▶ bodily-kinesthetic: "body smart"
▶ musical-rhythmic: "music smart"
▶ naturalist: "nature smart"
▶ interpersonal: "people smart"
▶ intrapersonal: "self smart"

Students may grasp new concepts more easily if they have opportunities to process the information in a way that makes sense to them and that comes most easily to them. The following list contains some indicators to help you determine at a glance some of your students' most developed intelligences.

### Verbal-Linguistic (Word Smart)

◆ loves language and words
◆ enjoys reading and writing
◆ is good at word games and puzzles
◆ uses metaphors and colorful language

### Logical-Mathematical (Logic Smart)

◆ creates logical patterns
◆ is good at strategy games like chess—often a competitive player
◆ enjoys numbers and calculations
◆ uses lists and step-by-step approaches

### Visual-Spatial (Picture Smart)

◆ can transform images easily to another medium, such as drawing, sculpture, construction
◆ has a vivid imagination and visualization skills—creates mental movies
◆ is interested in color, arrangement, texture, balance, design
◆ likes pictures, video, computers, TV

### Bodily-Kinesthetic (Body Smart)

◆ prefers to learn by doing
◆ likes to use the whole body to process learning
◆ might be an athlete
◆ might be a performer, a dancer, or an actor
◆ likes to construct and deconstruct

### Musical-Rhythmic (Music Smart)

- easily recognizes tones and rhythms
- often sings, hums, or taps when working and processing
- knows the words to many songs
- is sensitive to environmental sounds
- might play an instrument or sing

### Naturalist (Nature Smart)

- has sensitivity and connection to the natural world
- notices seasonal and other environmental changes
- recognizes patterns in nature
- works best outdoors or near a window
- likes to have plants and animals around

### Interpersonal (People Smart)

- communicates well
- enjoys working with and helping others
- is very social and has many friends
- can read others' intentions, moods, and feelings

### Intrapersonal (Self Smart)

- processes information and solves problems best while alone
- takes time for reflection and contemplation
- is independent and not very social
- has a strong intuitive sense

Many easily available surveys can be administered to students to help quickly identify some of their most developed intelligences (see the student checklist opposite), although their talents and gifts are usually apparent to an observant teacher or parent. Determining what intelligence area is a student's least developed might be more helpful. (Thomas Armstrong and others suggest that we avoid labeling a lesser developed intelligence as a weakness or deficit. It simply is an area that needs further development.)

# Eight Kinds of Smart
## Student Checklist

Name: _____ Date: _____

These intelligences are common ways in which people process information and solve problems. Which are your strongest intelligences, and which are your least developed? Check those statements that apply to you most often.

## Verbal-Linguistic: Word Smart

____ Books are important to me.

____ I have a pretty easy time memorizing poems, stories, facts, and so on.

____ I enjoy talking and telling stories.

____ I enjoy games like Scrabble, Boggle, and Hangman.

____ I like to write in a journal or write stories.

____ I like to look things up in books and encyclopedias.

____ I like to listen to people read aloud to me.

____ When I ride in a car, I like to read signs or play the A-B-C Game.

____ I enjoy tongue twisters, rhymes, and puns.

____ I like to use big words when I write or speak.

## Logical-Mathematical: Logic Smart

____ I enjoy counting things.

____ I like to make patterns, and I notice patterns in my world.

____ I often ask adults questions about how things work or about things in nature.

____ I can add and subtract in my head.

____ I like to measure, sort, and organize things.

____ I like to do games or solve problems that require logical thinking.

____ I am interested in new inventions and theories in science.

____ I like to set up experiments.

____ I enjoy doing math at school.

____ I like watching science shows or nature programs on TV.

## Visual-Spatial: Picture Smart

\_\_\_\_ I enjoy drawing and painting pictures and designs.
\_\_\_\_ I love colors, and I have some special favorites.
\_\_\_\_ I enjoy putting together puzzles.
\_\_\_\_ I like playing with blocks, Legos, Tinker Toys, and so on.
\_\_\_\_ I have vivid and colorful dreams.
\_\_\_\_ I can close my eyes and visualize things in my head.
\_\_\_\_ I can usually find my way around my neighborhood or town.
\_\_\_\_ I like to take pictures or videos.
\_\_\_\_ I love to look at picture books or magazines that have a lot of photos.
\_\_\_\_ I can pick and match clothes to create great outfits to wear.

## Bodily-Kinesthetic: Body Smart

\_\_\_\_ I play at least one sport on a regular basis.
\_\_\_\_ I find it difficult to sit still for long periods of time.
\_\_\_\_ I like working with my hands, doing activities like building, weaving, carving, and so on.
\_\_\_\_ I think I am pretty coordinated.
\_\_\_\_ I need to touch things in order to learn more about them.
\_\_\_\_ I love wild rides at the amusement park and other thrilling experiences.
\_\_\_\_ I often spend my free time outside.
\_\_\_\_ I like to ride a bike or skateboard or go skating.
\_\_\_\_ I enjoy dancing.
\_\_\_\_ I can act and imitate other people's movements.

*Teachers, Change Your Bait!* © 2005 Crown House Publishing Ltd. • www.CHPUS.com
Adapted from *Begin with the Brain*, by Martha Kaufeldt, © 1999 Zephyr Press. Used with permission.

## Musical-Rhythmic: Music Smart

\_\_\_\_ I have a pretty good singing voice.

\_\_\_\_ I can tell when someone sings or plays a wrong or off-key note.

\_\_\_\_ I like to play or would like to learn how to play a musical instrument.

\_\_\_\_ I like to listen to music on the radio or on a stereo or computer.

\_\_\_\_ I sometimes catch myself humming a tune when I am working or learning.

\_\_\_\_ I love to have music in my life.

\_\_\_\_ I like to tap or bang out a rhythm on things.

\_\_\_\_ I've made up songs.

\_\_\_\_ I notice nonverbal sounds (dog barking, waves, etc.) and hear things pretty well.

\_\_\_\_ I sometimes get a melody or advertisement jingle stuck in my head.

## Naturalist: Nature Smart

\_\_\_\_ I love nature, animals, and the outdoors.

\_\_\_\_ I can sense and notice patterns in nature, and I enjoy pointing them out to others.

\_\_\_\_ I am able to use patterns to navigate (get around), and I am not afraid of becoming lost in nature or a new environment.

\_\_\_\_ I am sensitive to the changes in seasons, moon phases, tides, star patterns, and so on.

\_\_\_\_ I am interested in learning the names and characteristics of various plants and animals.

\_\_\_\_ I enjoy watching nature shows and programs about exploration and other cultures.

\_\_\_\_ I find it fascinating, not frightening, to be in environments different from my own.

\_\_\_\_ I enjoy watching natural phenomena, like comets, sunsets, thunderstorms, and waves.

\_\_\_\_ I blend in easily within nature or a new culture; sometimes I even feel more comfortable in these situations than in others.

\_\_\_\_ I often want to be out in nature when I am thinking about something or solving a problem.

*Teachers, Change Your Bait!* © 2005 Crown House Publishing Ltd. • www.CHPUS.com
Adapted from *Begin with the Brain*, by Martha Kaufeldt, © 1999 Zephyr Press. Used with permission.

## Interpersonal: People Smart

____ I usually have an easy time making friends.

____ I am good at helping others solve problems.

____ I often want to help others.

____ I usually know what is going on with my friends and family (gossip!).

____ I am often a leader in clubs or cooperative learning groups.

____ I am the kind of person that others seem to come to for advice.

____ I prefer group sports to individual activities.

____ I like to play games with others rather than doing things on my own.

____ I feel comfortable in crowds and at social gatherings.

____ I think I notice when people are upset or having a hard time.

## Intrapersonal: Self Smart

____ I am pretty independent; I don't rely that much on others.

____ I have hobbies that I like to do on my own.

____ Sometimes I have opinions or ideas that set me apart from others.

____ I like to keep a personal diary or journal.

____ I would prefer to spend time alone in the woods than at a busy, fancy resort.

____ I enjoy playing games by myself (video games, solitaire) rather than with others.

____ I like to think about important ideas and my goals.

____ I need time to work on things by myself rather than in a cooperative group.

____ I have a secret place or fort that I like to go to in order to get away from others.

____ I sometimes have a difficult time talking with others in a small group.

Based on Gardner (1993) and Armstrong (2000, 2003).

*Teachers, Change Your Bait!* © 2005 Crown House Publishing Ltd. • www.CHPUS.com
Adapted from *Begin with the Brain*, by Martha Kaufeldt, © 1999 Zephyr Press. Used with permission.

## Learning Styles and Modalities

MI theory is a popular basis for understanding how individuals process information and solve problems. Another consideration is learning style or modality—how each of us prefers to gather information from the environment. Various instruments label students' particular learning styles. Gregorc, 4-MAT, and Dunn and Dunn are some well-respected, commercially available identification tools. Many of them could be helpful, especially if you have experience using them already. For instance, knowing whether a student is abstract random or concrete sequential could help you decide which lure to select from your tackle box. A simple understanding or review of learning modalities is a great place to start.

The basic modalities we use to acquire data are

- visual (see, read, observe)
- auditory (hear, talk, listen)
- kinesthetic/tactile (touch, do, participate)

Modalities can help us understand how each of us learns as well as how we deal with situations on a day-to-day basis. If someone tells me (auditory) what is to be done, I know that I might not remember. If I write it down and look at the list (visual), I know I am less likely to forget. Another person may want to rehearse what needs to be done, to try it out (kinesthetic). Doing it once first will be the key to remembering for them.

## Prior Knowledge and Interests

We know that the brain is shaped by experiences. If children have had many varied opportunities to create, build, travel, discover, play, and interact, their brains will be organized differently than children who haven't, and multiple connections will already be developed. When new concepts and ideas are introduced to a child who has prior knowledge, you can see the connections being made immediately. "Oh, I've done this before"; "This is just like when I went camping"; "My dad showed me how to do this when I was little."

Prior knowledge and experience jump-start learning. Without the brain connections to hook ideas to, many students feel lost or confused by new concepts. Checking for what most students already know about an upcoming lesson is key to knowing what lure you will need from the tackle box. As Jane Healy explains in *Endangered Minds,* "Without experiences there are no concepts. Without concepts, there is no attention span because they don't know what people are talking about" (1999, 41).

**DISCOVERING WHAT STUDENTS KNOW**

- Modify the All about Me survey. Include questions that relate to the unit to be taught. For example, before a lesson on fire and combustion, ask for responses to these items:

  ▶ Describe a time when you saw a campfire or bonfire or sat in front of a fireplace. What did you see, hear, or smell?
  ▶ List what you know about candles.
  ▶ Describe a time when someone in your family accidentally burned food in the kitchen. What happened?
  ▶ Have you ever gotten burned? Tell what happened. How did it feel?
  ▶ Draw a picture of a flame. What colors do you remember?

- Tell a personal story about an experience you have had. Encourage the students to share related stories and experiences in a class discussion.

- Read a newspaper or magazine article about a person or event that is related to the lesson coming up. Generate a discussion about the students' personal experiences.

- Create a simple questionnaire that students can respond to with basic answers, such as "yes," "sometimes or a little," and "never."

- Use novelty and humor. Wear a hat or costume or bring in a prop. See which students in the class know about what you have. Who is asking questions?

- Ask parents to respond to a question in the parent newsletter. They can generate a discussion with children at home to help refresh their memories.

In addition, the topic to be taught may be of particular interest to several students in the class. Science lessons often reveal who in the class is into airplanes and rockets, birds and reptiles, dinosaurs and fossils, and so on. I once taught a gifted fourth grader who listed his favorite author as Isaac Asimov! Most important, listen to students and observe their reactions. Taking mental notes about each student's varied responses should guide you as you develop the first strategies for introducing the concept to be taught.

Vary some of the learning activities to stimulate those children with prior experiences. When surveying students and during discussions, recognize who is experienced and capable around the topic. In addition, many textbook formats have pretests you can administer to determine which students have already mastered the concepts. Teachers often develop ways for students to show what they already know. When you determine that some of the students can already demonstrate competency and an understanding of the standards to be taught, create ways to expand and extend a child's interest. *Lateral enrichment* (page 95) and *compacted curriculum* (page 76) strategies are other key aspects of differentiated instruction.

## Identify Developmental Stages, Readiness, Challenge Areas, and Limitations

Adding to the problem of children's lack of prior experiences is the push for more complex concepts to be introduced at earlier grade levels. Since the 1990s, as the standards movement and high-stakes testing policies have come to dominate school planning and curriculum design, students at lower grade levels are being exposed to—and are expected to master—many skills and concepts that may be developmentally inappropriate. In a given class, only some students' brains may be ready to tackle more complex concepts. Other students will struggle with these challenge areas, but with differentiation and time, will eventually develop the ability to meet the challenge. Students with limitations may always require differentiation and additional help to learn certain concepts.

Our knowledge base is growing exponentially with technology, as information is discovered, reported, and shared instantaneously. How can we decide what kids should know? If we add more to the knowledge database, what can we omit from the curriculum? Educators are directed to teach more each year, and yet we are not given clear strategies for what we can now leave out.

If we return to what we know about the brain's developmental stages and sensitive periods, we have some guidelines for what we might expect from our students. As described in chapter 1, a teenager's brain is just beginning to think abstractly and manage complex thinking. No wonder teaching middle school can be such a challenge. Students in this age group have one of the greatest ranges of cognitive abilities (i.e., from one student to another).

Some general points to remember about various age groups:

**Preschool students (ages 3–5)**

- enjoy learning and are super curious
- are social but not always cooperative with others
- need lots of physical activity
- are ego-centric and live in the present
- can remember approximately two to three "chunks" of information
- can pay attention for two to six minutes
- need simple explanations

**Primary students (ages 5–9)**

- focus on single attributes at a time
- need lots of physical activity
- may worry about such things as imaginary monsters
- have difficulty with abstract thinking and understanding cause and effect
- focus on the here and now
- can remember approximately three to four chunks of information
- can pay attention for approximately six to ten minutes

### Intermediate students (ages 9–12)

- focus on multiple attributes at a time
- are most concerned about friends and acceptance
- have difficulty with abstract thinking and understanding cause and effect
- don't see the implications of actions
- focus on the here and now
- can remember approximately four to six chunks of information
- can pay attention for approximately ten to fourteen minutes

### Secondary students (ages 13–18)

- understand different perspectives and views
- seek individuality, autonomy, and recognition
- can think abstractly and understand cause and effect
- can focus on the "long ago and far away"
- can remember approximately six to eight chunks of information
- can pay attention for approximately twelve to eighteen minutes

## Physical and Language Limitations

Students' physical limitations or level of language proficiency will also guide how you accommodate students or modify the instruction to meet individual needs so that learners can experience success and participate as fully as possible. There are unlimited possibilities for accommodating students with hearing, sight, or mobility challenges:

- books on tape
- laptop computers
- PDAs
- calculators
- headphones or other audio enhancements and listening devices
- magnifying lenses
- personal assistants

To be successful, students learning English as a second language (ESL) may also need modified instruction. Making sure that resources are available in other languages is imperative for students needing to do research. Students may have prior experiences with the concept but not yet have the English vocabulary to demonstrate their understanding. When planning a unit or lesson, I always try to view it through the eyes of the struggling learners, gifted students, and non-English speakers to see if I can provide any adaptations to help every student be successful. Some modifications may need to be impromptu.

## Cultural Sensitivity

In addition to considering possible language differences, sensitive teachers must also review and consider cultural diversity. Our own unconscious biases and prejudices can often seep into how we organize our classrooms and instructional practices. Consider these questions about your own classroom:

- ◆ Are seating arrangements restricted or purposely exclusive to any students?
- ◆ Could comments about the modifications or accommodations made for language needs possibly be construed as put-downs?
- ◆ Might you be making assumptions about students' lack of prior experiences based on their socioeconomic, ethnic, or cultural background?
- ◆ Does a student's appearance have any effect on your interactions with him or her?

With information gathered about each student, you are now ready to review the curriculum and begin to differentiate instruction to fit the unique needs of your learners.

Collecting information on students can be done in a variety of ways. Some methods can be rather informal, such as discussions and brainstorming. Paying close attention to students' responses to questions will provide valuable information you need to plan instruction. More formal data gathering might include the use of prepared pretests or teacher-created surveys.

# Teacher down the Hall Story

In a seventh-grade humanities core class, I once taught transitional ESL students. The standards for that course included writing a short research paper and giving an oral presentation. I accommodated the students in many ways. I first made sure they had a wide range of choices for the research paper. The library and media specialist had assisted me by pulling together a special cart with books in Spanish on diverse topics and books in English that were written at several levels of difficulty. I had a part-time bilingual assistant who worked with the Spanish speakers to organize their thinking using graphic organizers and helped eventually with their translations into English. The ESL students also had a modified assignment. The paper had to include all the same organizational steps as other students were required to include, but the length was reduced.

Many students were anxious about the oral presentation—even the English speakers! There were clear expectations and multiple opportunities to practice with a partner. When one student, Miguel, got up to share his report on soccer, his favorite sport, he went catatonic. I tried to kill a little time for him and reminded the students about being good, patient audience members, but he was still at a loss as to how to begin. Then a caring, brilliant classmate raised his hand and asked me if the students could start by asking questions rather than waiting until the end of the report. Of course!

Students began to raise their hands, and Miguel would point to them to hear their questions. "When did you first start playing soccer?" "In Mexico, when I was little, my brothers and cousins taught me how." "What is your favorite team?" "Now it is the Earthquakes." The questions came, and Miguel answered. Because a few students had rehearsed with him, they started formulating questions that would lead him to his report. Miguel was smiling by the end, and I'm sure he felt very relieved. From then on, if a student requested it, the oral presentation could begin with a few questions from the audience. It was a minor modification that produced great results!

Individual student profiles can be developed. These might include inventories about a student's learning styles or multiple intelligence strengths. By determining each student's developmental stage, readiness, prior experience, challenge areas, and limitations, you will be better able to differentiate instruction.

## *Tackle Box Ideas*

- ◆ Conduct an All About Me survey that includes at least eight questions. Start a file for each student. (See the sample survey questions on page 19 if you need help getting started.)

- ◆ Survey students to determine their MI strengths and areas that need further development.

- ◆ Observe students carefully. Make notes about each student's cognitive and emotional thresholds.

- ◆ Reflect on your own possible biases and assumptions about students based on gender and language or socioeconomic, cultural, and ethnic backgrounds.

# 3
# Varying the Physical Environment

## In and out of the Classroom

▶ Consider the effects of environmental stimuli on the students' brains and bodies.

▶ Modify seating arrangements within the classroom to accommodate students' preferences.

▶ Investigate and use alternative work areas.

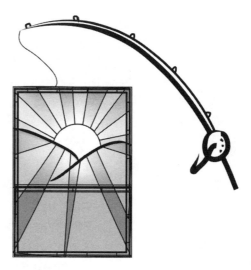

*S*ome *of the environmental elements scientists are examining include class size, furniture design, temperature, humidity, color, sound, movement, plants, air quality, aroma, and lighting. The most effective teachers are aware of the cognitive effects of these variables.* (Jensen and Dabney 2000, 27)

Sometimes the most basic and obvious differentiation techniques are the simplest to implement in the beginning. Perhaps you are already trying some of these strategies, such as modifying seating arrangements and work spaces. Where the learner is located within the classroom environment may enhance or inhibit his or her capabilities. Some seating changes may be obvious; other rearrangements may not at first seem necessary. This strategy may involve a trial-and-error approach.

## Consider the Effects of Environmental Stimuli

Before considering seating and work space strategies, we should understand the effects of the physical environment on the brain's functioning. Although we each are unique in our reactions to lighting, temperature, noise, and other environmental stimuli, we can pinpoint certain facts about how all brains react in common.

### Lighting

- ◆ Lack of natural, full-spectrum lighting can affect students' vision and increase eye fatigue. In addition, low lighting can increase drowsiness and decrease concentration levels. Mood changes and depression have also been linked to a lack of adequate daylight exposure.
- ◆ A learning environment that is dependent on fluorescent lighting has possible adverse effects on students' vision as well as potentially causing academic and health deficiencies, slower growth rates, and amazingly, even higher rates of dental cavities.
- ◆ Fluorescent lights have been linked to attention disorders, hyperactivity, and the triggering of headaches and seizures. The flickering vibration of the light quality as well as the audible hum may have additional detrimental effects.

*(See Hathaway et al. 1992; and Jensen and Dabney 2003, 11–13.)*

- ▶ Bright natural light is most conducive for learning. Leave curtains and blinds open if possible.

▶ Reduce the use of fluorescent lights by turning some of them off (or simply having the custodian remove a few bulbs). Enhance the lighting by using small bedside lamps with incandescent bulbs.

▶ Investigate replacing standard fluorescent bulbs with full-spectrum bulbs.

▶ Consider getting the class outside for a brief impromptu "field trip."

## Noise

◆ Behavioral problems, ADHD issues, and students being off-task can be a result of a noisy learning environment.

◆ Learning environments are often bombarded with white noise. Even students with normal abilities to filter out classroom sounds such as fan noises, air systems, computer stations and monitors, overhead projectors and lights often complain of being fatigued or having headaches from the constant noise.

◆ ESL students and students with hearing impairments or learning disabilities have a difficult time hearing the teacher and other students in a room with poor acoustics and ambient noise.

◆ Constant exposure to a poor acoustical environment may even hamper language skills and vocabulary development. Fewer than 10 percent of classrooms are likely to meet appropriate acoustical standards.

*(See Jensen and Dabney 2003, 24–26.)*

▶ Soften as many hard surfaces as possible in the classroom to reduce acoustical reverberation. Hang tapestries on walls and use area rugs on floors.

▶ Try to mask the white noise by playing quiet background music or using a small fountain or a fish tank to produce more natural, environmental sounds.

▶ Instigate schoolwide quiet times, when there are no intercom interruptions or outdoor maintenance (such as leaf blowers) allowed.

▶ Consider using an audio-enhancement system for your own voice. This would include a wireless microphone and a speaker system installed in the classroom.

## Visual Stimulation

- ◆ Color can affect moods and attitudes. Reds and oranges can stimulate creativity and energy but also may produce tension and not be particularly pleasing.
- ◆ Colors are more difficult to discern and identify in a poorly lit environment.
- ◆ The poor physical conditions of a school or classroom can have a negative effect on student learning and behavior and can promote absenteeism.
- ◆ Clutter can be visually distracting and promote confusion. Disorder conflicts with our brain's natural tendency to organize.

*(See Jensen and Dabney 2003, 15, 22.)*

- ▶ Organize shelves, materials, and displays to evoke a sense of safety and security.
- ▶ Blues and greens have a calming, relaxing effect and can increase alertness.
- ▶ Add color to displays, presentations, and handouts when possible
- ▶ Much of our brain is devoted to what we see. Much of what we learn and absorb comes from peripheral stimuli. If the stimuli are positive, important, and interesting, learning can be enhanced.

## Temperature and Air Quality

- ◆ Some researchers believe that reading comprehension, math skills, and the ability to perform physical tasks may decline if the temperature in the classroom is higher than 75 degrees (Fahrenheit).
- ◆ A room that is either too hot or too cold may be uncomfortable to students and distract from learning.
- ◆ A stuffy classroom may have an ionization count that is in the positive range (highly electrified), which may produce groggy, sleepy students—definitely *not* conducive to learning.

*(See Jensen and Dabney 2003, 8–9, 31–32.)*

▶ Good air circulation can improve learning by enhancing alertness and relieving stress.

▶ A constant room temperature of 68–72 degrees (F) will enhance learning for most students.

▶ A pleasant-smelling classroom can reduce anxiety and encourage engagement.

▶ Consider using a room ionizer to enhance the air quality.

## Basic Needs

◆ When students perceive that water, food, and bathroom privileges are restricted, they may feel anxious and irritated even at the thought of not being able to meet their own basic needs, such as getting a drink when needed.

◆ Dehydration has been linked to poor learning and appears to contribute to stress levels.

◆ Needing to move around, get fresh air, stretch our legs, take a break, and so forth are all natural responses to extended learning periods.

*(See Kaufeldt 1999.)*

▶ Basic physical and psychological needs must be satisfied for the brain to be able to focus on complex tasks (Kaufeldt 1999, 73). Only when we are satisfied can we attend to the business of learning or recreating.

▶ Some students may find a rocker or beanbag chair more comfortable than sitting at a desk or table for long periods of reading or studying.

Knowing how students might react to various stimuli in their physical environments should influence how you differentiate instruction. What might at first appear to be an attentional disorder, a learning disability, or a behavioral problem might have its roots in *where* the student is expected to learn. Investigate a few modifications in seating, location, and environmental conditions before trying more complex differentiation strategies.

## Modify Seating Arrangements

Flexible seating arrangements can make a real difference for some students. When a student's behavior, attention, or learning seems affected by something, take a moment to consider the environmental stimuli near the student.

- Is the lighting bright enough? Is it natural or fluorescent?
- Is there too much ambient noise near the student? Is the student near a heater or air-conditioning fan? Near an overhead projector? A computer? A noisy student?
- Is the classroom temperature a consistent 68–72 degrees (F)?
- Does the student have a view that is not too cluttered or distracting?
- Could some procedures be created that allow for students to get a drink or use the restroom as needed?
- Have you asked the student about location preferences? For example, "Is there a place in the classroom where you might be more successful?"

## Create Alternative Work Areas within the Classroom

In my classrooms I have always tried to have a Take-Five area for five-minute rests—with no questions asked. It is usually a rocker or beanbag chair near a lamp or plant in a corner of the room. Classrooms are often crowded, and furniture is lacking, but consider arranging low bookcases, file cabinets, or tables to create more comfortable, intimate spaces. Younger children especially love forts. By placing a table against the wall with a couple of foam cushions or pillows on the floor beneath it, you can create an instant reading nook. Use a clip-on lamp for appropriate lighting. I also tried to have a table at the back of the room where students could work with others. Consider other possibilities:

- Is there a different chair or a cushion you could introduce?
- With procedures in place, could students sit on the floor?
- Could you provide some clipboards for writing when not at a desk or table?
- Could students bring in pillows on which to sit?

## Investigate and Use Alternative Work Areas

I always find it interesting how divided teachers are on this issue. Some feel that any common space in the school should be available for students' use, with appropriate supervision. Others *never* let students out of their classrooms. They feel that they are intruding or overstepping boundaries if they let the learning overflow outside the room. I believe that with procedures in place and reasonable expectations, many of our students can benefit from being away from the four walls of the classroom. Take time to investigate possibilities and brainstorm with colleagues about common expectations.

- ◆ Could a couple of students work just outside the classroom door if it is left open?
- ◆ Is there an adjoining coat room, office, or storage closet that could be converted into a study cubby?
- ◆ Is there a commons area in which a small group might meet for short periods of time with little supervision (within range for the teacher to hear and see what's going on)?
- ◆ Could students work outside the classroom on a bench or their own chairs?

## Collaborate with Other Teachers

Many opportunities arise when teachers take time to collaborate and plan with each other. This includes grade-alike and subject-alike colleagues, but also means coordinating with resource teachers, specialists, and library and technology teachers. With prior arrangements made, it may be possible to send a few students to another teacher for short periods of time to work on specific tasks or projects.

- ◆ Are there times when a resource specialist might have workspace available in a tutorial lab or resource room?
- ◆ What agreements can be made for sending groups of students to the library?
- ◆ If your school has a technology lab, could some students work there independently for short periods of time?
- ◆ By prior arrangement, could one or more students work in another classroom?

## Teacher down the Hall Story

*O*n occasion in my classes I have had a student who is a constant source of disruption to others. The student isn't always misbehaving; he or she just needs to move more, talk more, or get reassured more often. Sometimes I would determine that the rest of us needed a break, and I would ask the student to take a note to a fellow teacher. The note might say, "Don't send him back!" The other teacher and I would have previously agreed that the one receiving such a request would keep the student there to help or to work in her classroom for a specific amount of time, such as twenty minutes. We called this the *Lend Law*—I can lend you one of my students from time to time and you can lend me one of yours as needed. The break often gives the class a chance to refocus, and classmates are more tolerant of the student when he or she returns.

If we are going to differentiate instruction by *beginning with the brain,* then a careful assessment of the learning environment should come first. Research is determining that many physical aspects of a classroom appear to have a real impact on learning. If modifying lighting, noise, and temperature can help even a handful of our students be more successful learners, then what is stopping us from giving it a try?

### *Tackle Box Ideas*

- ◆ Survey the classroom. When students aren't present, sit in various seats in the classroom and observe the physical environment from their perspectives.
- ◆ Investigate alternative seating possibilities; create a Take-Five area.
- ◆ Collaborate with other teachers and specialists about the possibilities for students working outside the classroom.

# 4
# Varying the Social Environment
## *Flexible Grouping*

▶ Establish a sense of
belonging and inclusion
by creating base *tribes.*

▶ Pre-arrange various
partnerships and small
groups to save time and
reduce stress.

▶ Identify *learning clubs* as
needed to reteach or to
cluster students based on
interest.

*The brain's capabilities are enhanced by positive social interaction. One's own identity and the ability to learn are profoundly influenced by noncompetitive interpersonal relationships and one's feelings of inclusion in a social group.* (Kaufeldt 1999, 59)

When we consider differentiating instruction in the classroom, some of the most important tools we have available to us—for free—are the other students. Knowing one can ask questions of peers, feeling supported by classmates, and having opportunities to get feedback from other students are all benefits to students who work with one another. Organizing pairs and establishing groups in advance can save incredible amounts of time later. Creating a system for forming random partnerships can also come in handy. For students, knowing ahead of time whom they will be working with can relieve anticipatory anxiety.

### ANTICIPATORY ANXIETY

When the brain perceives a threat in the environment, experiences confusion, or feels anxious about possible activities coming up, the body may go into the reflexive response in *anticipation* of the stress, not because of it. Some students seem to exhibit this response more often and easily than others. Knowing what the game plan is and how things will be done ahead of time helps the student stay engaged in the task rather than obsessing over anticipated details.

## Create Tribes

*Tribes are formed sociometrically to distribute boys and girls, students of high and low peer acceptance, and people of heterogeneous abilities. . . . People are seated together in a small circle or square of desks, or at the same table. Unlike many cooperative learning approaches being used in schools today, Tribes stay together over a long period of time. . . . The size of the Tribe varies depending upon the age of its members and its purpose. . . . The power of being included and valued by peers motivates students to active participation in their own learning.* (Gibbs 1995, 22)

I have successfully used strategies from the tribes model for years. One idea that I have routinely used, with a few modifications, is the concept of forming a base group to which a student is usually assigned for the whole year (or semester). At the beginning of the year, after students have had a chance to meet and work with everyone in the class, I let them submit the names of three to five students with whom they know they could work well. I create base groups of four to six students and try to balance the following characteristics when assigning the teams.

- leaders
- problem solvers
- boys and girls
- energy levels
- backgrounds and languages
- cognitive abilities
- creative and artistic talents

Once the tribes are announced, I orchestrate various activities to build inclusion and a sense of belonging. The tribes should have some tasks or a project that they could do together. After an initial period to establish their relationship, they do not have to sit with each other all the time.

You could use the tribes for various purposes:

- Students meet with their tribes at the beginning of class to take attendance.
- Tribes collect and distribute homework, papers, and so forth.
- When students return from an absence, their tribe-mates provide them with information about homework and what was done in class.
- Tribes sit together at assemblies.
- Tribes are buddies on field trips and in carpool arrangements.

Being a member of a tribe builds a sense of belonging and inclusion, which leads to feelings of safety and security. Over time, members begin to count on each other and build almost familial bonds. Students get to know well the others in their groups, learn patience and compromise skills, and experience

**Resources**

For further details on how to set up tribes, see Gibbs, *Tribes: A New Way of Learning and Being Together* (2001) and www.tribes.com.

the caring within the group. Having pre-established tribes when differentiating instruction enables you to arrange students quickly into small groups for various activities.

## Pre-Arrange Various Partnerships and Small Groups

Students benefit from working with a peer at many points during the learning process. When a teacher describes an activity, students often ask, "Can we work with somebody?" If the answer is yes but the partners aren't predetermined, the next few minutes become a free-for-all as students scurry to get paired up, wasting valuable time. To save time, there are several ways you might have students already organized into partnerships or small groups, such as triads or larger. Be sure to include a chance for students to work with friends on some occasions.

### Process partners

I use this term to describe students who sit next to each other and can discuss or work together quickly and efficiently. A process partner differs depending on where a student is sitting at the time.

### Peer editing partners

These are predetermined partners with whom students work whenever they need to edit their writing. By working with the same partner over a period of time, students can develop rapport and give more accurate feedback.

### Clock partners

Distribute a copy of the clock partners reproducible (page 47) or have students draw a clock face. Each student will collect the names of other students for each numeral on the clock face. If Greg puts Lynn down as his three o'clock partner, Lynn records Greg's name at the same time. I usually let students select a few of the partners themselves. I assign some of the pairs to help make sure students are with compatible partners. For instance, I will organize the students into peer editing pairs based on their writing abilities so that they are each partnered with someone who is working at about the same level. I will have all students in the class write down the name of their peer editing partners at six o'clock. Then whenever I need students to write together or review written work, I can ask them to look at their clocks and remember who their six o'clock partner is and meet with that person.

### Compass partners

As a variation of clock partners, I use a compass rose. This has nothing to do with actual locations. The directional points are just where students write in the names of their designated partners; for example, a student's north partner might be Rick and his or her south partner might be Pat. Often, I assign the east partner for a particular reason but let students choose a friend as the west partner, which they love.

### Three's a charm

For a few activities, it is beneficial to have a group of three students work together. Three is also best for conflict-resolution processing, with one student serving as a mediator.

### Numbered heads

In my classes, I prefer to have students sit in table groups of four to six. (If you don't have tables, a cluster of desks or a row of students can be designated as a group.) Within this small group, each student has a permanently assigned number. I can easily give procedures for activities and designate roles and responsibilities to the various team members by using these numbers. See the example in the box below.

Reel Good Idea

---

**FIELD TRIP FUNDS BRAINSTORM**

Tell students they have ten minutes to come up with ways the class could raise some money for a field trip, working in their small groups. Each group records everyone's ideas, then presents at least three ideas to the class. Each person in the group has a responsibility:

- Timekeeper: Number 1
- Summarizer/Reporter: Number 2
- Recorder: Number 3
- Encourager: Number 4

---

By having prearranged numbers within each group, you can easily select other subgroups.

Other ways to use numbered students:

- ◆ "I would like all Number 4s to come to the back table with their assignments."
- ◆ "Ms. Lambdin needs a few helpers in the library. Would the Number 2 person from each group please go with her now."
- ◆ "There are materials for this activity over on the shelves. I'd like the Number 1s to get the supplies for their groups."
- ◆ "During this next work time, if you have a question, please ask the Number 3 person in your group first for help."

### That's my color

Assign each student a color as well as a number. Make sure that students with the same number aren't also the same color. For example, Number 2s are not also all Greens. In the same way as with numbers, you can now designate roles and responsibilities or direct students to participate in something. I use the colorful sticky dots used on files to distinguish student colors. These can be put on students' name badges on the first day of school, then on papers to be passed out to each group. This is especially helpful when I am *jigsawing* a task (such as having each group member learn a different piece of information before teaching the group what they learned on their own; see page 69). If the table groups have even numbers of students, I can use the colors to pair students together within the group, such as having blues work with greens.

### Peer helpers

Before any work time begins, ask students if a few would like to serve as advisors or peer helpers. In some classes, this is a source of pride and status. In other classes, the task sometimes seems burdensome. If several students volunteer, let them! If no one volunteers, encourage a few to take a turn at it—not just the gifted students, either. I keep on a hook old conference badges that hang around the neck. I print them with things like "Writing Helper," "Math Master," and "Ask Me How. I Know What to Do!" Some teachers worry that a less-than-capable student might offer to be a helper. Sometimes that

**Resources**

Try using a spinner to make selections seem random, such as Spencer Kagan's Student Selector for the Overhead Projector, available at http://www.kaganonline.com, or by calling 1-800-933-2667 (USA and Canada); 949-369-6310 (international)

happens. My experience with this is that that student loves wearing the badge and that the other students either avoid asking that student or can figure out fairly quickly if the "help" is correct or not.

**PEER EDITING AND FEEDBACK CIRCLE FOR POETRY**

Have students arrange their groups clockwise in this order—blue, red, yellow, green. Ask them to read each student's poem and write a comment on the poem or on a Post-it. Allow two minutes per poem, then ring a chime or bell. When the chime rings, students pass the papers to the people on their left. This is a reflective and intrapersonal activity. Limit talking.

### Quotation Club Meeting

**Who:** Anyone who needs a little more help with quotations.

**When:** During writer's workshop time for the next three days.

**Where:** At the back table— bring materials.

## Orchestrate Learning Clubs

Frank Smith first described learning clubs in his book *Insult to Intelligence* (1986). They are small groups that can comprise students who have similar needs or interests. The groups might meet for instruction or to do research together. They can be used for short-term ability grouping for reteaching a particular skill or concept. They could also be used as long-term groups, such as a literature study groups. Students are particularly receptive to learning clubs when the membership changes at intervals. As students master skills, they may be regrouped into different clubs. I use learning clubs also for *invitational help,* as illustrated.

# Teacher down the Hall Story

I regularly invited students to be members of flexible learning clubs that I designed for reteaching difficult skills or concepts. Instead of posting or calling out the names of students who needed extra help, I would encourage students to decide for themselves if they thought they could use some review and reteaching. I would give students some assessment criteria to use in making their own decisions: "If you noticed when you got your paper back that there were four or more items marked incorrect, then you probably could use a little review and jump-start. I'd like to invite you to the back table for a quick learning club time."

As students got help and were feeling more successful, it became known that learning clubs were good things—not punishments or consequences. Students were being given another opportunity to be successful. Even though membership in a club was encouraged to be voluntary, I would sometimes print up some invitations to pass out to certain students who might benefit from meeting with the other club members. Some students still needed the extra nudge. I also believe that many students don't know what they don't know.

In every class there were a few students who would come to almost every learning club I organized. If it was for reteaching or extra help, they would still show up, even if they were already competent. I found that many of them used the small group club format as an opportunity to do a little grand-standing, showing off what they already knew. I kept trying to let the clubs have self-selected membership, but these few kids were always making the struggling students feel inadequate.

We finally made a rule that if the learning club was for reteaching and a student already knew the skill or concept, he or she was welcome to attend and help but couldn't "let the cat out of the bag." These students started becoming terrific assets to the clubs. They would ask leading questions, give terrific examples, and really take pride in helping the other students get it.

Learning club possibilities:

- ◆ literature/novel study clubs
- ◆ jigsaw clubs (see page 69)
- ◆ review clubs (those who need reteaching for mastery or tutorial)
- ◆ above-and-beyond investigation clubs
- ◆ rotation centers (see page 110)

When you are beginning to implement differentiated instructional strategies, arranging students into various partnerships and small groups can take up valuable time. In addition, if students don't know each other very well or haven't worked with each other before, then the task or activity might be compromised by a lack of relationship. Students who feel connected to multiple groups and partners will begin working much more quickly when they are asked. By establishing base groups, or tribes, all students will have a circle of peers they can count on and will develop a sense of belonging. This feeling of inclusion within the class will maximize learning.

## *Tackle Box Ideas*

- ◆ Arrange students into base tribes and orchestrate initial inclusion activities, such as any variation of the Name Game or People Hunt ("Find someone who . . ."), or have students share something they cherish, favorites, or other personal details with other members of their tribes.

- ◆ Assign colors and numbers to students to aid in spontaneous flexible grouping.

- ◆ Create systems for students to get help from each other individually (peer helpers) and in small instructional groups (learning clubs).

# 5
# Varying the Presentation
*Hooking Students' Interest*

▶ Use novelty and humor to engage students' attention.

▶ Link the new concept or skill to the here and now and to students' daily lives.

▶ Orchestrate a discovery process using a project, an experiment, and technology resources.

*E*motional arousal is an indication that something important has occurred or is about to occur. But where? To find out, our emotions activate a complex cognitive system that selects and temporarily focuses on key emotionally important elements in an often confusing environment and maintains goal-directed behavior in highly distractible situations. (Sylwester 2000, 29–30)

In differentiated instruction discussions, much emphasis has been placed on varying the content of the curriculum, the process of learning, and the student products. I believe that first and foremost, however, teachers need to evaluate their own presentation strategies and make sure they vary them regularly. Direct instruction of a lesson is only one way to deliver information to students. Often key vocabulary, a concept, or a skill is best presented first by the teacher before the students do any types of activities to process understanding.

If you know that a lesson will work best if begun with direct instruction, be aware that children's brains have individual limits for maintaining sustained attention. It has been estimated that, in general, there is a one year to one minute correlation for children's attention spans, give or take two minutes. An average 12-year-old, therefore, might be able to attend to your presentation for 10 to 14 minutes. Of course, this is true only if the student is well rested, has had proper nutrition, and is not on any medications; it may be diminished if the student is coping with an attentional disorder.

Keeping in mind students' attention spans, consider orchestrating *how* new information is presented to students to be a high priority. Differentiated instruction can begin with a good introductory lesson. Knowing more about the brain can help you get the learner's attention, make the information relevant, and hook new concepts to the here and now.

## Use Novelty and Humor

*Attention: The selection of stimuli to which we direct conscious thought.* (Smith 2002, 195)

Getting kids' attention has always been a central goal of educators. In his book *A Celebration of Neurons* (1995, 78), Robert Sylwester describes four abilities that an effective attentional system must have: "An effective attentional system must be able to (1) quickly identify and focus on the most important items in a complex environment, (2) sustain attention on its focus while monitoring related information and ignoring other stimuli, (3) access memories that aren't currently active, but that could be relevant to the current focus, and (4) shift attention quickly when important new information arrives."

Our sensory systems are constantly scanning the environment for stimuli. When something unexpected happens, such as a sudden movement, a loud noise, the appearance of an interesting object, or any major change in the environment, the brain focuses attention on it. The attentional system was designed to be on alert for possibly dangerous situations, but the brain's persistent interest in novelty is not limited to threatening situations. If the brain is in a predictable, repetitive environment, then interest is lowered and the attentional system may continue to scan for new stimuli. Students who are in classrooms where the routine is always the same and the presentation and activities are repeated each day may seek out additional stimulation. Often if students are required to stay seated and quiet, the stimulation they seek will be generated from within, such as by daydreaming. For some students, determining if they can drill a hole in an eraser with their pencil point becomes a fascinating challenge!

You can capitalize on students' novelty-seeking brains. By varying your presentation strategies, using visual aids, and incorporating curious events, you can easily capture students' attention every day. I remember the surge of excitement that my classmates and I would feel when the teacher would wheel in the movie projector for a special presentation. The A.V. monitor would load the fragile film as the curtains were drawn and lights turned off. In classrooms 40 years ago, the anticipation of something different such as this was a classic attention getter. Students today are not as easily amused. As our multimedia-based technology has developed, even children in poverty often have TVs and VCRs available to them. In classrooms, the use of overhead projectors, videos, calculators, intercoms, and cable TVs has become common.

## MAKE ME LAUGH!

*Humor is by far the most significant activity of the human brain.*

*—Edward de Bono*

Our brains love a good laugh. There are physiological, psychological, sociological, and educational benefits to using humor in the classroom. As long as the humor isn't sarcastic or a joke at someone else's expense, opportunities to laugh should be included in every lesson. A funny story, a pun, or a clever trick will get the brain's attention quickly. Gaining students' interest and attention as you begin a lesson is imperative.

Some other benefits of using humor and laughter in school:

- Laughter and smiling cause the release of endorphins in the blood. It is our natural pleasure chemical. We feel euphoric and enjoy the moment.
- When we laugh with others (not at them!), we bond and form a sense of inclusion.
- Since emotions can enhance retention, laughing will increase the chances of students remembering what they learned.
- A good laugh can relieve stress and tension. This can lighten students' mental attitudes and lessen the chances of them giving up or feeling frustrated.

"Children have become accustomed to these rapid sensory and emotional changes, and respond by engaging in all types of activities of short duration at home and in the malls. By acclimating itself to these changes, the brain responds more than ever to the unique and different—what is called novelty" (Sousa 2001, 28). Sousa adds that schools haven't changed much in what they offer as an engaging environment. High school classes still often involve lectures. Whiteboards may have replaced blackboards, but the overhead projector is still often the most high-tech tool in a classroom. We are up against brains that have developed a high threshold for novelty.

A few novel ideas:

◆ Bring in real props and examples that can be passed around and examined.

◆ Wear a hat or costume that relates to what will be learned.

◆ Start with the ending! Do the activity first (see the discovery process on page 58).

◆ Play an audio recording of a famous speech, a hit song, animal sounds, or anything relevant.

◆ Orient the classroom a new way, such as by changing the seating to face the back of the room.

◆ Walk around, stand on a chair, speak with an accent—make them look at you!

◆ Tell a joke.

◆ Learn a magic trick.

◆ Interview a "guest speaker" on a speaker phone.

◆ Without the student's knowledge, arrange ahead of time for a parent to call you on your cell phone during class and ask to speak with the student to say, "Keep up the good work!"

## Link the New Concept or Skill to the Here and Now

So much of the stated curriculum seems to be anchored in the "there and then" and the "long ago and far away" that relevance to the learner is difficult to find. I believe that everything is connected, and with careful review, you can find a link to your students' world. It's a shame when we don't take the time and thus miss a valuable opportunity.

Teachers will argue that the stated curriculum insists they teach a unit such as the rain forest at a particular grade level. I understand the pressure, and I believe it is our responsibility to discover the overarching concepts (essential understandings and key points) in the unit, then find a connection to something in the here and now for the students—something that is relevant to their own area and daily lives. Start with that connection, using it as a springboard to the required unit. Help the kids see the relevance and significance of studying the topic.

**For example:**

| REQUIRED UNIT | | HERE AND NOW CONNECTION |
|---|---|---|
| Westward Movement | → | Why students' families moved here |
| Meteorology | → | Local weather patterns |
| Geography and Land Forms | → | Maps of the local area |
| Influential People in History | → | Local heroes |
| Inventions | → | Everyday things in our homes |
| Architecture | → | Local buildings |
| Ancient Cultures | → | First local residents |
| Rivers and Oceans | → | Local pond or creek |
| Economics | → | Getting a part-time job |

# Orchestrate a Discovery Process

Rather than starting with information you present to the students, what if they were to discover key points on their own? What a concept! With some careful planning and preparation, you can create an activity that engages learners' attention and at the same time helps them learn processing skills. Although these kinds of activities could be done as independent tasks, why waste a great opportunity to orchestrate some partner or group work?

**DISCOVERY PROCESS**

An engaging activity that ultimately leads students to discover key understandings is central to the *discovery process.* Students may discover more than you anticipate, and therefore the activity need not be a task with step-by-step directions. This type of activity might begin with a question to be answered, a hypothesis to be tested, an object that needs to be identified, or a structure that needs to be built. The key is that students' active participation in the learning increases their chances of storing the new information in long-term memory.

## A Teacher down the Hall Story

My son participated once in an incredible unit at school on the Amazon rain forest. The teacher provided information from scientists working in the Amazon. The students "sold" rain forest for one dollar per acre to raise money to help conserve the region. They each researched and studied a different animal from the area, then built models of the animals and put them together into an Amazon Rain Forest Experience at school. At open house, parents would pay a quarter to get a guided docent tour through the realistic display.

My son cleverly assembled a papier-mâché model of a blue and gold macaw in our garage and then brought it to school with great pride. Most of the students were engaged and excited by the project. They learned a lot and professed a strong commitment to saving the endangered species and forests in the Amazon basin.

The day after the project was complete, a couple of the students got in trouble in our neighborhood for breaking a branch off a neighbor's tree and chasing her dog. Had the important concepts (save trees and protect living things) taught in the school unit eluded the kids when they were at home? The answer is yes! I call this a missed opportunity. If only the teacher had started the unit with an article from our local Santa Cruz newspaper. In our area we constantly have issues with our beautiful redwood trees and the lumber companies. We also have the Monterey Bay, with endangered species of whales, elephant seals, fish, pelicans, and so forth. The students know little of these issues but are now experts on the Amazon rain forest.

**Resources**

I have used many of the
GEMS units and FOSS
science kits from the
Lawrence Hall of Science
at the University of
California, Berkeley.
They all emphasize the
discovery approach and
inquiry method of
learning. Find out more
about their products at
http:// www.lhsgems.org.

Activities that involve experiments, construction, dissection, investigation, and so forth are perfect for the discovery process. For example, you might have students individually read a passage from a novel, resource book, or newspaper first, and then form small groups to determine motive, form opinions, discuss alternatives, and anticipate what will happen next. The groups' opinions and answers could then be shared with the class.

Some of my favorite discovery process activities:

- Dissect a single rose bud (or any flower blossom) and draw it at various points along the way, using a magnifying lens for the examination.
- Build tall towers using plastic drinking straws and straight pins.
- Build card houses using a deck of playing cards.
- Determine how much water a disposable diaper can hold until reaching saturation.
- Dissect turkey, pig, or cow hearts (or other parts, such as lungs, kidneys, or eyes).
- Use a magnifying lens to burn stuff—supervised, of course!
- Mix food coloring in small cups of water or experiment with watercolor paints to create different colors.
- Watch worms or snails move on glass.
- Make fingerprints and compare with others.
- Make oobleck (cornstarch and water mixed into a very thick paste) and discover its unusual properties.

When wrapping up the discovery process activity and identifying the concepts that were discovered, also take time to ask and discuss questions about the process:

- Did you ever feel like giving up?
- Did anything unexpected happen?
- What part surprised you the most?
- What would you do differently next time?
- How should I [the teacher] set this up differently next time?

Varying the presentation of new material to students is an essential element of differentiated instruction. Capturing their attention by using the brain's attraction to novelty and humor is where you should start. Upper grade teachers especially need to watch the amount of direct instruction. Balance how long you talk to kids with their age-range ability to pay attention. Whenever possible, consider starting a lesson with the discovery process. Orchestrate opportunities to let students experience the learning process firsthand. I assure you that the lightbulbs coming on over their heads as they have an "Aha!" moment will be incredibly satisfying.

## A Teacher down the Hall Story

One of my favorite discovery projects is in *River Cutters*, a GEMS teaching guide (Sneider and Barrett 1999). A middle school class I taught started a unit that was to include river systems, water pollution, erosion, geological landforms, flooding, reservoirs, and human impact on watersheds with the *River Cutters* experiments. Using diatomaceous earth (often used in swimming pool filters), straws, plastic cups, and water, the students created a drip system and built a model of an active river. Within one class period, these middle school students understood erosion! Each day that they set the system up, the results were varied. Using books, illustrations, and guides provided with the unit, they soon knew about tributaries, deltas, and alluvial plains. Many students asked if they could stay in at break to continue working on the projects. After several days of experimentation, I served as a summarizer of what was learned.

### *Tackle Box Ideas*

♦ Observe how much time you spend giving direct instruction. Limit the number of minutes you talk based on how old the students are.

♦ Make the presentation of new material interesting, exciting, and humorous. Bring in a prop or curious objects to launch the lesson.

♦ Select a unit that might be able to start with a discovery project. Avoid giving too much information or vocabulary or too many key points to the students first—let them be investigators!

# 6
# Varying the Content
*Meaningful, Specific, and Appropriate*

▶ Emphasize meaningful, relevant, and worthwhile content to motivate and challenge students.

▶ Engage students by teaching specific areas in depth rather than broad general concepts.

▶ Adjust the curriculum to match and accommodate students' readiness levels.

*P*erhaps most significantly, studying topics and facts as information to be memorized fails to engage the deeper intellect of students. When students are encouraged to think beyond the facts and connect factual knowledge to ideas of conceptual significance, they find relevance and personal meaning. When students become personally and intellectually engaged, they are more motivated to learn because their emotions are involved. They are mind-active rather than mind-passive. (Erickson 2001, 20)

Successfully designed curriculum is a wonderful combination of relevant, meaningful *content* that is *processed* by the learner in various ways to build understanding that can be demonstrated through a range of *products.* Curriculum content is difficult to separate from the processes and products, but each element can be varied in its own way. When creating differentiated instructional strategies, look to each element for possibilities. (See chapters 7 and 8 for discussion of the other elements, process and products.)

## Emphasize Meaningful, Relevant, and Worthwhile Content

As chapter 1 details, a key element of brain-compatible learning is the exposure to and interaction within a multisensory-enriched environment. When children have had developmentally appropriate play and problem-solving experiences, their brains have the necessary wiring started to make connections when new concepts are presented. An enriched environment doesn't mean *overstimulation*—flash cards for babies, super-achieving preschools, or an overscheduled summer—it means normal opportunities for children to play, experiment, make mistakes, build things, take things apart, get wet and dirty, laugh, get frustrated, create, imagine, and daydream.

Children who have limited exposure to the world due to poverty, institutionalized care, disabilities, or even a dependence on TV and technology may not have the beginning hooks in their brains to connect new learning. When doing experiments or activities that involve water, for example, teachers often see who has had previous experiences playing with water: bathtub play, creek play, hose play, and so forth. When doing measurement activities to develop math concepts, it is usually obvious which students have used a tape measure before or have measured ingredients for a recipe. I brought in a standard broom to illustrate a stage I lever. Many students didn't know how to use this "nonelectrical" dustbuster! This lack of prior experiences with real-world objects may also contribute to students' difficulty with reading comprehension. If one hasn't had an experience or observed something similar, then it may be difficult to create a mental movie, which is what we do when we comprehend what we are reading. When you introduce a concept, you may need to provide more hands-on discovery activities than originally planned. Many upper grade teachers report that students seem clueless about topics that used to be well grounded. Rather than blaming these students for their lack of background, we should be better prepared to integrate firsthand experiences within the instruction to get everyone on board. Of course, this means more *time*, both to prepare and to implement in the classroom, but this planning and preparation time is well worth the effort. Students are able to grasp concepts and skills easily when provided firsthand experiences. As teachers, we save time down the road by not having to reteach.

## The Search for Meaningfulness

*In order for students to exert maximum effort, they need to understand that the work being completed and the information being studied are meaningful.* (Erlauer 2003, 55)

Whether or not something is *meaningful* is personal and determined by the learner. As discussed in chapter 5, teachers want to present new information as *relevant* to the students' daily lives. The new knowledge must seem pertinent to their everyday lives and experiences. When the learner's brain has the opportunity to recognize the new skill or concept as being *important* and having a *purpose,* then it is more likely to connect the new idea to prior experiences. Individual meaning is influenced by and is a result of how students relate the content to their past experiences. If they have limited prior knowledge and experiences, helping them attach meaning to new learning may be more challenging.

"Fortunately, the brain sifts through all incoming sensory stimuli and selects those that are the most relevant or meaningful" (Wolfe 2001, 103). Our brain's networks of prior experiences are formed throughout our lifetimes. Incoming information that connects to an existing network has a much better chance of being processed and stored than information that is previously unknown or perceived as irrelevant or useless. If our goal is to have students become engaged learners, we must create ways for the curriculum to be perceived as meaningful, relevant, and important—that is, worth doing!

> *"A meaningful curriculum is characterized by high interest and high relevance and it taps into learners' feelings and experiences"* (Tomlinson 1999, 19).

When you take time to get to know your students, you are better able to make the curriculum meaningful. When I present workshops to teachers all over the country, I try my best to find out important, interesting, and even playful tidbits about the region that I can insert into the presentation. I try to get some details about local current events and issues by talking with anyone I can, including the taxi driver and hotel front desk clerk. I make sure to read the local newspaper. By acknowledging a difficult election that just happened or the success of a local sports team, using regional terminology and geographic locations, I can hook my key concepts to the participants' daily lives and experiences. In order to differentiate the instruction for my students in the classroom, I make it a point to find out what is important in their daily lives:

- What music are they listening to, and what artists are the most popular?
- What sports and teams, if any, are important to the students, their families, and the community?
- What places in the neighborhood are visited often, revered, and known to all?
- Who are some important local heroes and well-known people?
- What TV shows, movies, videos, and DVDs are they watching?
- What current issues are important to the community?

# Teacher down the Hall Story

One year while serving as a teacher coach, I planned a lesson with a middle-level social studies teacher. He was frustrated with the U.S. history textbook he was using and the overwhelming amount of Revolutionary War trivia he was expected to teach. We made it our goal to create relevancy and meaningfulness and still teach the content.

He was supposed to teach about the Quartering Act of 1765, when colonists were ordered by the British government to provide shelter, food, supplies, and weapons to the British soldiers. On the day of the lesson, the students were surprised to hear the teacher say that the administration was cutting back on basic school supplies but had approved that teachers could take any necessary items from their students. He demanded that a couple of students (secretly arranged ahead of time) dump out their backpacks and purses on their desks, and he proceeded to collect any pens, highlighters, and miscellaneous supplies that he wanted. The other students were surprised, alarmed, and very defensive.

"You can't just take stuff from us!" "This is my private property—this is illegal!" "Don't even try to get into my backpack!" He continued his charade and also told them that on the weekend, he and his family needed a place to stay while their home was being painted. He claimed that the school administration had approved that he could stay at any student's house because he was a state employee. He would be coming to someone's home that weekend and staying and eating. Again, the protests came from students.

"You've got to be kidding!" "No way!" "My dad's got a gun!" The whole class was engaged, emotional, and claiming that he simply couldn't do it. Many, of course, were smiling and wondered what he was up to—he had captured their attention, for sure.

The students were asked if they were sure that the teacher couldn't do this. What laws were there to protect their families' privacy? Could you defend your home with a gun—legally? As students jumped into a lively discussion, they were steered to their assignment. What laws do we have to ensure each person's right to protect his or her private property? In addition, they were going to investigate current laws about schools' rights to search student lockers.

Later these students were cleverly assigned the task of analyzing how the Quartering Act may have influenced the writing of the Bill of Rights and Constitution. We had come up with a relevant, meaningful situation to hook students' interest and then were able to compare the situation to something in the past.

If your instruction includes comparisons, examples, and references to aspects of the students' daily lives, they are more likely to pay attention and hook the new information to what they already know and have experienced firsthand.

**INTEGRATED AND INTERDISCIPLINARY CURRICULUM**

For thirty years (yikes!) I have been a strong proponent of designing integrated thematic curriculum units. I know the brain responds to the connectedness of ideas and likes to see the whole picture. If we continue to design departmentalized, fragmented curriculum, kids will end up with several separate puzzle pieces and may not understand how the new information fits into the real world.

By reviewing the standards, you can look for meaningfulness, for relevancy, and then orchestrate the new information around a central theme or guiding question. Tasks and activities would involve crosscurricular connections. Doing a research paper might involve content area standards, language arts skills, technology, and collaborative work on a project or performance. In secondary classrooms, teachers can coordinate across subjects to create interdisciplinary units. An integrated culminating assignment might be turned in for a grade in several classes.

## Engage Students by Teaching Specific Areas in Depth

To provide meaningfulness and encourage engagement, avoid teaching general survey courses that give just an overview of the topic. By studying a topic in depth, one can feel like more of an expert. Learning details is more interesting and engaging than getting a general overview.

In this way, you can choose a particular lens through which to look at a particular topic. When studying immigration to California, for example, we used three views of why particular groups might have chosen to come to California. Need? Greed? Or curiosity? Some immigrants came to our state to escape persecution or slavery, or they needed employment or education that was unavailable in their own country. Many folks originally came to California for gold. Later, lumber, oil, agriculture, and Hollywood were all potential millionaire makers. Over the years many folks came just because they were risk takers or simply curious. By limiting the perspectives, students were able to categorize immigrant groups into the three possible motivating reasons for immigration. We used the motivation categories throughout the year to look at immigration on national and worldwide scales ("What motivates people to leave their countries and move to a new place?"). Of course, we started the unit with discussions and a graph relevant to students: "Why did your family originally move to Santa Cruz? To California?"

When faced with the daunting task of having to teach about several ancient cultures, I often choose to do an in-depth study of one of the cultures with the whole class. Then I arrange students into ancient cultures study groups. Each group is responsible for researching a culture and presenting that research to the class. I use the standards and essential understandings to guide my lessons, trying to focus big ideas into manageable pieces without getting lost in factoids.

When studying about different cultures and civilizations, I use a list of the *cultural universals*—things that all cultures have in common—to help guide my selection of what to emphasize (see page 70). All might be interesting, but I will choose just two or three to have students investigate.

## Jigsaw Areas of the Curriculum

The jigsaw strategy can be used in two effective ways. One way focuses on process and is discussed in more depth in chapter 7. The other way focuses on content. The students start assigned to a base group. Each member of the group goes to a different table or area to meet with other students. (This is a great time to use the colors or numbered heads strategies described on pages 48–49.) At each of the different table groups, there is a task, reading, or activity related to a particular key point or concept of the topic. At the end of the activity, students return to their original groups and are responsible for teaching or sharing what they learned at their jigsaw table. In other words, they each bring back a piece of the puzzle to share with the group. Students feel a sense of responsibility and relief that they don't have to do everything on their own!

## CULTURAL UNIVERSALS

The characteristics we use to identify and compare cultures throughout time are *cultural universals.* These are customs and practices found in every culture, to varying degrees, worldwide. The only difference is that each culture expresses each custom or practice quite differently.

**Basic needs:** All cultures need to meet the basic needs for survival—food, shelter, clothing.

**Geographic location:** What they use to meet their needs will be based on the region where they are located.

**Tools and technology:** Cultures invent tools to assist and improve life in their environments.

**Communication and education:** All cultures develop ways to communicate in order to pass on valuable information.

**Family structures:** All cultures develop a family or kinship organization.

**Belief in the unknown:** Cultures create religions, rituals, and stories to explain life, death, and other concepts not easily explained.

**Artistic expression and leisure:** Cultures develop music, dance, rituals, and artistic representations.

**Government:** As cultures and tribes get larger, a system of governance is created and monitored.

**Trade and economy:** Ultimately, as a culture creates or finds an abundance of a resource, it seeks ways to trade with other cultures for items to improve the quality of life.

Adapted from Murdock (1945).

When covering the curriculum seems overwhelming, divide up some of it, assign it to several expert groups, and jigsaw for a longer period of time, ending with presentations to the class. The groups will need some guidelines for what to include in their presentations. The students will also need to know in advance to what degree they will be responsible for learning the material that the others have presented. Many content areas of the curriculum lend themselves well to jigsawing. I have used this method to study novels by the same author or novels that represent a particular style or theme.

Topics that jigsaw well:

**Ancient cultures:** Greek, Roman, Mesopotamian, Mongolian, Egyptian

**U.S. geography:** Northeast, South, Midwest, Southwest, Great Lakes, West Coast

**States of matter:** gas, solid, liquid

**Rocks and minerals:** quartz, volcanic, sedimentary, aggregate, slate

**People who have made a difference:** Martin Luther King, Jr.; Franklin Delano Roosevelt; Thomas Edison; Susan B. Anthony

**Endangered species:** pandas, whales, wolves, condors

**Inventions that changed the world:** wheel, printing press, gun powder, internal combustion engines

**Import products to the United States:** petroleum, coffee, beef, clothing, bananas, technology

When using the jigsaw technique, first model for the students what the expectations will be. I usually do this by leading a whole-class investigation of an important aspect of the larger topic. In this way I can demonstrate for the students a pattern for what their small groups eventually will do.

*Reel Good Idea*

## ELEMENTARY JIGSAW EXAMPLE

When teaching an elementary unit on birds, lead the class first in an in-depth study of a local bird. Include key points: What does it eat? What kind of nest does it build? Does it migrate? What does it look like as a baby and as an adult (male and female)? Does it have enemies? Is it endangered? Create various activities and research for the students to do on the same bird. Arrange a chance for them to see the bird in its environment if possible.

Then have students request another bird to study in a small group. (I usually supply a short list of other local birds that will be investigated.) Have them submit their first, second, and third choices. Assign students to these research groups using good judgment about the group's overall makeup. Give an assignment task sheet, and orchestrate research and work time. Announce when the presentations will be done and what the requirements will be for completion, as shown in the example below.

## BIRD STUDY GROUPS

By Wednesday, May 12, have the following completed and be prepared to teach the class about your selected bird in a five-minute creative presentation. Include

- a colorful drawing of the adult bird on 12" by 18" paper
- a chart, using pictures and words, of what the bird eats
- three key points about and a drawing of the type of nest the bird builds
- a map of your bird's migration pattern *or* a map of where in the state the bird is found
- five additional interesting key points about the bird, for example: Does it sing? Does it swim? Is it endangered?

# Adjust the Curriculum to Students' Readiness

The best differentiated instructional strategies are pointless if used to teach useless information. When students ask questions such as "Why do we have to learn this?" and "When are we ever going to use this?" educators should find viable answers and present only concepts that they can make relevant. It's a shame when innovative teachers waste valuable time designing creative activities to teach concepts that are developmentally inappropriate.

## The Flow Zone

Individuals learn best when there is a moderate challenge in a low-threat environment. For the learner, there must be a balance between the appropriate skills needed and the challenge at hand (Csikszentmihalyi 1990). Students must feel as though they have at least a chance of being successful. If the task seems too difficult for the learner's perception of his or her capabilities, frustration will take over, and the reflexive response will keep the learner from going on. Motivation is lost. On the other hand, if the task is too simple for the learner's skill level, or the learner already knows the information, boredom will set in, and again motivation is lost. When orchestrating learning for all students, we must recognize what the appropriate level of challenge will be for each student.

Mihaly Csikszentmihalyi describes this *flow zone* in his book *Flow: The Psychology of Optimal Experience* (1990, 74). When applied to classroom practice, enhancing student flow means orchestrating powerful learning experiences based on every student's unique needs and abilities *and* continually reflecting on whether the task is too difficult and promoting frustration and anxiety or is too easy and promoting boredom and lack of motivation. If students are into the flow zone, when it is cleanup time you will hear, "Oh, no! Do we have to stop? Can't we keep going? Will we keep working on this tomorrow? Please?"

# ORCHESTRATING FLOW EXPERIENCES IN THE CLASSROOM

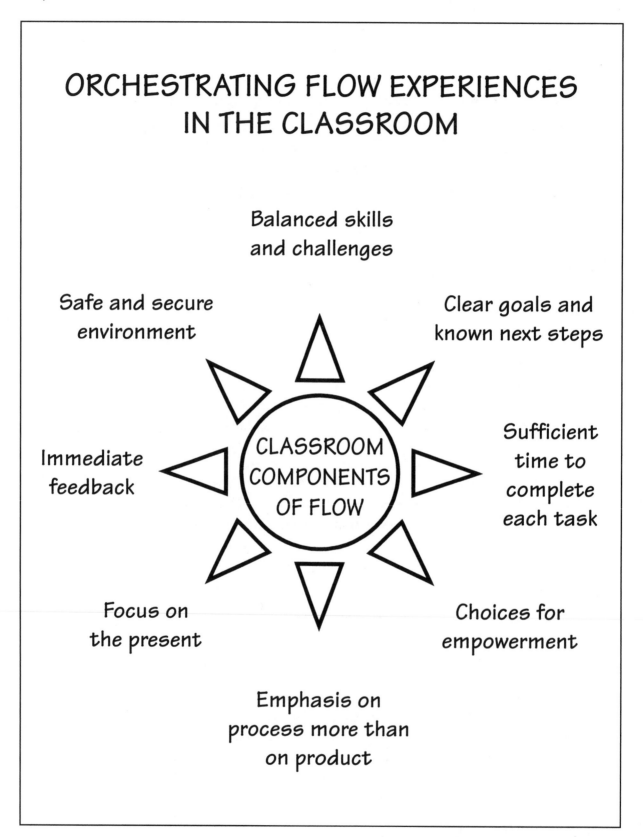

Balanced skills
and challenges

Safe and secure
environment

Clear goals and
known next steps

CLASSROOM
COMPONENTS
OF FLOW

Immediate
feedback

Sufficient
time to
complete
each task

Focus on
the present

Choices for
empowerment

Emphasis on
process more than
on product

Grade-level curriculum used to look different. In many districts, topics traditionally taught at upper grades have sifted their way or been pushed down to the lower grade levels. Concepts that are more abstract and conceptual rather than concrete and experiential will be difficult for younger learners. The frontal lobes of the brain do not fully kick into gear until the onset of puberty. When functioning properly, these areas are in charge of understanding cause and effect, time, and abstractions, and of conceptualizing ideas that aren't in the here and now (see more information on pages 29–31).

Standards-based curricula are often filled with factoids and concepts to be mastered at each grade level. *If the concepts to be learned at a particular grade level are developmentally inappropriate for that age of learner, then no matter how creative and differentiated the instruction is, the learner may be incapable of fully understanding the idea.* For example: space, planets, and the solar system used to be an upper-grade science unit, often emphasized in fifth or sixth grade. As we have discovered more about our solar system and beyond, the content of the unit has grown exponentially. If we teach about super novas and black holes in space in the upper-grade unit, then something from the space, planets, and solar system unit needs to go somewhere else. Often units on the planets, sun, moon, and stars are introduced to students as early as kindergarten and first grade. Although the students are able to memorize the names of the planets and make cute mobiles out of paper plates, actual understanding of orbits, rotation, seasons, gravitational pull, and the Earth's axis is a challenge for most six-year-olds—maybe even for many thirty-year-olds!

Is the concept too big to swallow? My point is that we should limit how much time and energy we use in developing differentiated instructional strategies for concepts that are developmentally inappropriate. When fishing, it is obvious that using a four-inch-long spoon lure would be ludicrous if you were trying to catch an eight-inch blue gill. Occasionally you will have one or two students who are functioning at a different developmental level and may get the concept, but don't keep throwing out the larger lure and then blame the little fish for not biting. Change your bait to something they can handle!

## Tiered Activities

Use *tiered activities* when you want to make sure all students focus on the same essential understandings and skills even though they work at different levels appropriate to their individual capabilities. The central task or activity is relatively the same for all students but may have modifications for both struggling learners and more capable students. (More examples of this as a differentiated *process* are described in chapter 7.)

Use the following basic format to create tiered activities:

1. Design a project, activity, or task that you want all students to complete.
2. Determine what parts of the project are non-negotiable—that is, parts that all students must do.
3. Arrange various levels of difficulty and complexity for the task. Keeping different students' ability levels in mind, provide different versions of the original task along a continuum of challenge. This could be as simple as two or three different levels, or you could provide several challenges and give students some choices.

## Compacting Curriculum

A common-sense approach in modifying the content for gifted and more capable students is to stagger where the student might start the lessons and compact what will be included. Students who are years ahead of their classmates often become frustrated when they are held accountable for all the daily requirements that are unnecessary to increase their own learning. Always having to do what everyone else is doing can be boring and can lead to a lack of motivation and a disenchantment with school. This particular one-size-fits-all approach seems to dominate in classes where a single textbook is the focus of the learning.

Compacting existing curriculum is a way to reduce the amount of redundant work a student must do and to provide exciting opportunities to expand and enrich the mastered learning. Many students have had prior experiences and developed competency in a particular lesson, activity, or subject. They could demonstrate mastery on the test or adequately complete an alternative form of assessment prior to the concept being introduced in class. It is common sense to give these students some type of replacement material they could work on instead of insisting they cover material they already know.

In general, organizing compacted curriculum is a three-step process:

1. Determine the standards, objectives, and key points that will be taught during this unit or lesson.
2. With preassessment strategies, discover which students already know about the topic and determine what skills and concepts each identified student still needs to learn and extend.
3. Create a meaningful compacted learning plan for these students that allows them to continue their study of the topic without starting at the beginning.

Teachers often find it easier to create *compacted groups.* In this variation, students with similar strengths, talents, and degrees of mastery can be clustered and work on a similar compacted plan. Students can actually apply to be part of the enrichment group and can join it by demonstrating understanding during a preassessment. By using groups, you have fewer individualized plans going on and the students have a peer group with whom to work. (For more on this type of *lateral enrichment and expansion,* see chapter 8.)

> Just as teachers have experienced the frustration and the challenge of adjusting the curriculum for students who experience difficulty in learning, frustration also exists when we realize that for some students, a good deal of the material that is being taught has already been mastered, or could easily be mastered in a fraction of the time that may be required by other students. Discomfort inevitably develops for both teachers and students in these situations.
>
> —Sally M. Reis and Joseph S. Renzulli (2004)

*Reel Good Idea*

---

**MATH EXAMPLE**

Before I introduce a new skill, concept, or lesson in math, I use a preassessment (often supplied in textbook programs) to determine which students have already mastered the concepts. Those who can demonstrate understanding at the beginning shouldn't have to go tediously through the early lessons. I cluster these students (into a learning club, as described on page 50) and create a compacted, modified instructional plan. (See the individualized math contract opposite.) I meet regularly with this learning club to discuss, assess, and extend what they are doing on their own.

---

## Vary the Resources

Another way to vary the content is to vary the way in which students are exposed to the new information. A student who might take a long time to read from a textbook might easily understand the information if it is presented in a video. My son recently finished his eighth-grade American history class by watching and discussing *Forrest Gump*. It was amazing the details of the twentieth century that he was able to comprehend when it was orchestrated and presented by a creative teacher and a popular movie.

Reading diary entries from settlers traveling over the Oregon Trail might inspire learners much more than a summary in a lecture. Researching new therapies for Parkinson's, Alzheimer's, or epilepsy using magazines such as *Discover, Scientific American*, and *Newsweek* may motivate some students. Having live TV broadcasts available brings the world's troubles and celebrations directly to our classrooms.

Technology has become a valuable tool for educators. Internet searches, links to other students all over the globe, and the ability to write to and get responses from real people in a short time (or even in real time!) are all huge opportunities for teachers who wish to get content to their students in interesting ways.

# Individualized Math Assignments

Name: _____ Date started: _____

Math standard/concept focus: _____

| Assignments | To be completed by | Done |
|---|---|---|
| 1. _____ | _____ | _____ |
| 2. _____ | _____ | _____ |
| 3. _____ | _____ | _____ |
| 4. _____ | _____ | _____ |
| 5. _____ | _____ | _____ |

To demonstrate your understanding of this concept, create two word/story problems. Illustrate the problems and then record your answers on the back.

1.

2.

Student signature: _____

Teacher signature: _____

Parent signature: _____

Since before the recent turn of the century, many teachers have been grieving the loss of thematic integrated curriculum projects and units. As they adapted previous content to the new standards, it often became fragmented and compartmentalized. Standards are written to the various subject areas. When we attempt to meet the standards, we often lose sight of the big picture. Many students find the curriculum irrelevant and meaningless. As described in this chapter, some of the students are also arriving to school with a lack of prior experiences. This double whammy for the kids should inspire educators to investigate the curriculum content in a new way. With a little adaptation and planning, you can make the "what" that needs to be learned meaningful to all students.

## *Tackle Box Ideas*

◆ Commit to jigsawing the content in at least one unit of study.

◆ Find a way to link the here and now to whatever you are studying.

◆ Avoid teaching generalizations. Try to go in depth and let the students become experts on a topic.

◆ Design a tiered or compacted curriculum plan to address the needs of your most capable students.

# 7
# Varying the Process
## *Making Sense of and Storing New Learning*

▶ Include diverse reflection activities to build long-term retention.

▶ Orchestrate frequent opportunities for choice using various intelligences and systems.

▶ Use available technology resources to gather information and integrate student understanding.

*P*rocess means sense-making or, just as it sounds, opportunity for learners to process the content or ideas and skills to which they have been introduced. When students encounter new ideas, information, or skills, they need time to run the input through their own filters of meaning. As they try to analyze, apply, question, or solve a problem using the material, they have to make sense of it before it becomes "theirs." This processing or sense-making is an essential component of instruction because, without it, students either lose the ideas or confuse them. (Tomlinson 2001, 79)

During learning, *processing* means making sense of new incoming information. It is an individual and personal endeavor; each of us will arrive at a different level of understanding. It involves time to run the new ideas through our brain's filter and see how they connect to prior knowledge. Processing should be a time when students *build* their understanding rather than having to *demonstrate* it. This is the time when real learning takes place, and yet it is often the piece that many teachers neglect to orchestrate.

I once had the opportunity to hear Linda Darling Hammond, author of *The Right to Learn* (1997), present at an international educational conference. She commented that when educators rely on the "sage on the stage" approach to teaching, they are simply doing "spray and pray"—that is, verbally casting out the information and hoping that it lands on fertile minds. She commented that if the spray-and-pray teaching method is used, then the most we can expect from our students are "sit and spit" responses. If we lecture to students or expect them just to read the chapter and answer the questions at the end, then we haven't really considered learning as an *active process.* Learning involves the brain, the emotions, the whole body—and time!

We should vary how students initially take in and process new information and then orchestrate opportunities for continued processing of skills and concepts to ensure long-term retention. As students take in new ideas, they should have multiple opportunities to try different processes that enable them to internalize and consolidate the information in personal ways, that is, to make a connection in the ways they learn best.

Once the initial understanding has begun, active processing continues to be the key for students' brains to file new concepts into long-term memory. Educators must have a full tackle box of ideas to help students process new learning. Just as when fishing, we should first choose our best lure—the one we think will work with this type of fish. If the learner has difficulty getting the concept, then we may want to consider changing the bait. Based on individual student needs, we may decide that an alternate process would be beneficial.

The flexibility required for changing bait doesn't always come easily to teachers. We often continue presenting ideas, skills, and concepts one certain way to the students for long periods of time. When they don't get it, we keep getting more and more frustrated. We blame their lack of learning on their behavioral problems, language needs, learning disabilities, TV and computers, last year's teacher—and, of course, the parents! We keep saying things like

> "Let me go over it one more time."
> "I'll try another example."
> "Try to pay attention this time."
> "Watch what I'm doing, so you can get it."
> "Sit up straighter, so you can pay attention."

When using your first "tried and true" approach, how long should you wait before changing your bait? In my experience, if I have presented new information using a particular process, and I have gone over it or redone it up to three times, then it's time to change my bait. Those students who could have gotten it in the way in which it was presented *got it already.* The others are waiting for you to change your bait. An even better approach is to anticipate that you will need several different process approaches to a new concept and present them in an integrated way, or at least one right after another, right at the beginning of the lesson.

## Include Diverse Reflection Activities

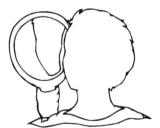

*Working memory is a temporary memory, so items have a limited time for processing. But the longer an item is processed (or rehearsed), the greater the probability that sense and meaning may be found, and therefore, that retention will occur.* (Sousa 2001, 66)

Learning and remembering new information takes time. Once a new concept has been introduced to and recognized by the brain, it must be processed and rehearsed a number of times and in various ways to ensure that it will be transferred to our long-term memory. So how long does it take? One memory researcher at John Hopkins University discovered that in

# Teacher down the Hall Story

It is often a struggle to teach upper-elementary students about using quotation marks when writing dialogue. One year, I was frustrated with my lack of success in teaching this skill. I had used a language arts workbook with practice lessons. I had run off additional workbook pages from a supplemental book. I had done review work on the overhead projector. I was getting modest results at best.

Because I knew that I had a number of bodily-kinesthetic learners, I had them start doing sentence strips with a pocket chart. Each word of the sentence and each punctuation mark was printed on a separate card. The cards were mixed up, and the students would then organize them on the table or on a pocket chart. This activity gained a little more involvement. The unmotivated students were at least a little interested in the novelty. We morphed the activity into a fun movement activity by hanging the words or punctuation marks around several student necks. One student would have to arrange the students in the correct order, left to right.

Although the movement, student engagement, and variety helped a few more students understand when to use quotation marks, I still needed another approach. I used my old Victor Borge videotape for inspiration. One of Borge's audience's favorite bits was when he would read a classic piece of literature, such as Shakespeare, and demonstrate a gesture and sound effect for each punctuation mark. A period was a noisy pop made with his mouth as he made a sharp jab with his pointing finger. Quotation marks were two curved fingers up in the air, making a little hook movement as he made a click-click sound—kind of like a giddy-up.

First with the whole class and later in our reading groups, whenever anyone had to read something out loud, different students would assume responsibility for a particular punctuation mark and jump in with the sound and gesture whenever it appeared in the reading. Needless to say, this novel process really helped many students put it all together. I believe that because of their active involvement, they had to pay close attention and couldn't help but notice, and begin to anticipate, where the correct punctuation should go. By changing the process for learning quotation marks, mastery was possible for all students.

Later in the year, as the students were taking a quiet standardized test, one student made the click-click sound we'd used for quotation marks. Everyone cracked up and knew exactly which question he was probably on!

healthy adults, it takes about five to six hours to consolidate a newly acquired motor skill into our brain's memory system. This is without any other new skills being introduced within the five hours, because that could slow the process down. (Sousa 2001). Many believe that a 24-hour time span should occur. It appears that much of our new learning gets filed into long-term memory when we sleep (Sylwester 1995).

**LOSE IT OR CONFUSE IT**

Without various opportunities to process new information, and without enough time to allow transfer into our long-term memory, the chances of quickly *losing* the new concept are great. It's not even that you simply *forget* the new information—it wasn't stored as a memory to begin with. You can't forget something that you never even learned! In addition, the research indicates that if too many new ideas are taught in too close a time frame, the brain may actually *confuse* the new concepts. This crosswiring may be at the root of some of the learning problems many students are demonstrating as teachers are pressured into teaching more, faster.

In a standard 50–60-minute class period, the peak learning time is the first 20 minutes (Sousa 2001, 88–89). Right at the beginning of a lesson, teach new information using a clever direct instruction, a discovery process, and quick reflections, and students will have greater retention. During the next 15 to 20 minutes, the brain will be ready for additional reflection time and activities to process the new concepts. The last 15 to 20 minutes are also important for the learner to have guided activities that will help *chunk* information and begin processing to determine sense and meaning. (*Chunking* occurs when our brain perceives a set of facts or data as a single item. It is a valuable memory tool if we can organize bits and pieces of new learning into a new "set." This is when our brain no longer sees the individual pieces of the puzzle; it recognizes the picture being made.) Times will vary depending on the age and attention span of the learner (see pages 30–31).

## Process Partners

When new information is introduced, the learner will need multiple, diverse opportunities to reflect and process. Some activities can be done independently, but collaboration with peers to review, discuss, and build understanding is a great technique. The strategy I use most frequently, with all age groups, is a simple reflection discussion with a process partner.

When I am presenting new information, I pause every few minutes and have students discuss what they are learning with a pre-established process partner. I might give a prompt or a question to launch the conversation. Sometimes I direct which partner should share first. By taking just one to two minutes to reflect quickly, students have the opportunity to

- ◆ recall what was just presented
- ◆ orally summarize the lesson
- ◆ listen to someone else's opinion and understanding
- ◆ be prompted to get their attention back to the lesson

### REFLECTION PROCESS

Any activity through which the brain recalls a concept, skill, or process is *reflection.* Reflection through *visualization* means creating a mental movie or picture of what was just said, done, or experienced. Reflection through *reproduction* means drawing, building, or designing a model or illustrating in some other way what was just introduced. Reflection through *journaling* means writing down thoughts, questions, and observations about the lesson. Reflection through *discussion* means talking and listening to others talk about the lesson. Any of these activities will prompt the brain to restimulate the new connections among the neurons, which helps strengthen them.

It is often said that neurons that fire together, wire together. Restimulating the initial brain connections ensures that the learner will have a greater chance of retaining the information for the long term and will be able to access it in the future.

## Independent Reflection Activity
## Examples for Students

- Write a journal entry to put new ideas in your own words, ask questions, or tell what the ideas remind you of.
- Draw a picture or diagram to illustrate the concepts.
- Use a graphic organizer to illustrate ideas and chunk information.
- Mentally rehearse or review what was just said or what it sounded like.
- Visualize and create a mental movie to remember what it looked like.
- Write a song or jingle to remember the steps involved.
- Create a hand jive rhythm to help emphasize the process used.
- Write down questions you have.
- Create an exit card by writing down three things you learned or thought about during the lesson and give it to the teacher on the way out (see page 155).

### *Journals*

Using a journal to reflect on a recent learning activity can be encouraged at any age, with minor modifications. As long as learners can hold a pencil or crayon or use a keyboard, they can transfer their ideas to the pages of a journal. In primary grades, a journal may comprise single pages on which students record words, sentences, or pictures. The pages are bound together later to form a booklet. Often a sentence prompt or frame will help the student focus the response.

**JOURNAL IDEAS FOR YOUNGER STUDENTS**

- Draw a picture or write a sentence about something you saw on the field trip today.
- Draw a picture or write a sentence about what happened when we tried to play the new game during P.E.
- Draw a picture that shows or write a sentence about doing a favorite activity today.
- Finish this sentence and illustrate it: "When we did the experiment today, I noticed that _____ ."
- Finish this sentence and illustrate it: "When I wrote my story today, I liked _____ ."

For older students, I use spiral notebooks or theme books. There may be more than one type of journal going in the same class. I like students to have a daily journal where they can free-write for about ten minutes to encourage general reflection about emotions, physical health, relationships, challenges and successes, and worries. This type of reflection encourages the learner to build up fluency in writing with a stream of consciousness approach. In class, I emphasize that these are *response* journals and that I will be looking at them and writing brief responses in them from time to time. They are not designed to be personal diaries with private information in them, although students are encouraged to create a journal for that purpose if they wish.

Responding to journals can be an overwhelming task, especially at the secondary level, when teachers may have more than 150 students. In a self-contained classroom, I try to take time each day—at lunch or after school—to read quickly and respond briefly to at least one table group's (or tribe's) journals. When I have several classes a day, as in middle and high school, I rotate so that each class gets a read and response from me at least every one to two weeks. (For example, I read half of first period's journals on Monday, the second half on Tuesday, and I continue through all my classes this way before returning to first period.)

**JOURNAL IDEAS FOR OLDER STUDENTS**

- Create a Mind Map of the key points of the lesson—use graphics!
- Recall a real-world situation where this concept (idea, process, or other) might be useful.
- What would you do? Describe how you think you might have reacted if put in a situation like the one we discussed.
- Create a simple flow chart to show how this new process is supposed to work.
- Create and illustrate a timeline of the events that were highlighted during the lesson.

Other journals may be more specific for different subjects. I have used math journals and asked students to reflect on how they approached a problem, what questions they had, what they learned in doing the problem, and so forth. Literature journals might have separate sections to record opinions about books being read, the titles of books that students have heard about and would like to read, and thoughts or feelings they have while reading a particular book.

### Interactive Notebooks

When directly instructing or demonstrating for students, I rarely let them just sit there and listen. I model for them ways to reflect by encouraging them to take notes on the lesson, using a graphic organizer or an interactive notebook. For younger students and students just learning to take good notes, I try *guided note taking*, where they copy ideas that I put down on an overhead or a chart as I am speaking (see the example opposite). They do not need to copy the words or graphics exactly, but instead they are encouraged to be creative and personalize the notes. With more experienced note takers, I might begin the lesson by asking them to get out their interactive notebooks and follow along on their own.

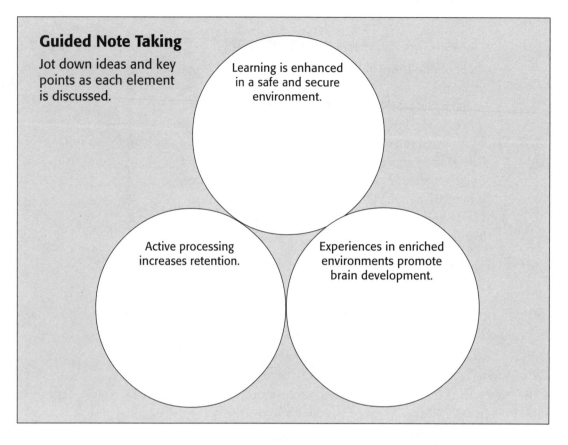

**Guided Note Taking**

Jot down ideas and key points as each element is discussed.

Learning is enhanced in a safe and secure environment.

Active processing increases retention.

Experiences in enriched environments promote brain development.

I often incorporate opportunities to develop Mind Mapping skills. These can be guided at first, and later the students can develop their own graphics and style. When studying about the early explorers of California, I used the mind map shown on page 91 for note taking. The first example (left) was photocopied and given to each student. In addition, I made a transparency of the same page to use as I gave information about the reasons that California was so popular to explorers (right).

I organized the information around three G words—gold, glory, and God—trying to use something catchy to help students remember the information. As I wrote with a pen on the overhead transparency, the students copied down the words and drew either my graphic or one of their own. When we were discussing the three G's, a student suggested we add globe as a fourth G word. It made perfect sense and we did! All students were engaged, participating, and learning.

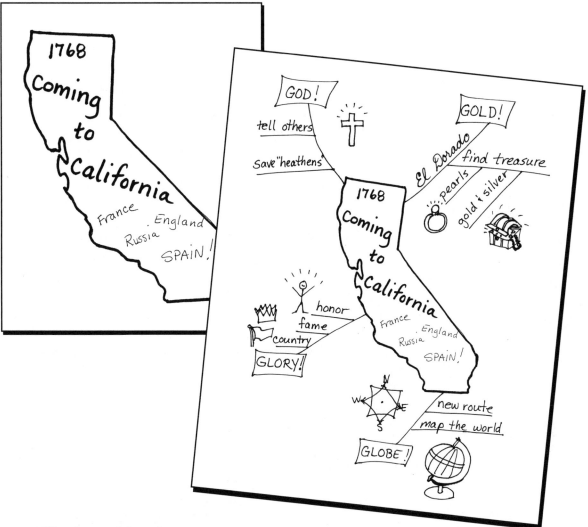

### *Reflection with Others*

Students can learn so much from each other. Orchestrating frequent opportunities for students to work with others can accomplish more than individual reflection can on its own. Getting together with other students, even for short periods of time, also enables students to

- ◆ move around a little bit, stand up, or sit on the floor
- ◆ practice the art of negotiation and compromise
- ◆ demonstrate social skills by being good listeners and speakers
- ◆ review, process, reinforce, and clarify new ideas
- ◆ benefit from hearing others' opinions and understandings
- ◆ build responsibility for and ownership of the learning process

Having pre-established groups and partners and well-designed procedures in place will help make collaborative reflective processing easier to orchestrate. (See pages 46–49 and 133–35.) Design most of these process groups to be short term and to help build understanding of a new concept. Don't issue grades for the group work, although you might check off students for participation.

*Reel Good Idea*

---

### COLLABORATIVE REFLECTION ACTIVITY EXAMPLES FOR STUDENTS

- Quickly review and discuss with process partners (see page 86).
- Brainstorm other possibilities and extend the ideas.
- Record ideas on a T chart (two columns formed from a large T drawn on a piece of paper, used for lists or brainstormed ideas using two criteria, such as listing the positives and negatives of an idea).
- Make a PMI chart and fill it in (see page 93).
- Reteach the new concept by explaining it to a partner.
- Take a side on an issue and prepare to share your opinions with the class.
- Individually share your opinion about or personal experience with an issue.
- Work together on a part of the new information (jigsaw) and be prepared to share your new learning with the whole group (see page 69).
- Share predictions about an experiment or project that will be conducted.

---

Another guideline to help us think about processing time comes from David Sousa (2001), based on work from noted educator Madeline Hunter in the 1980s; Sousa explains Hunter's terms *massed* and *distributed practice.* Massed practice means students try different examples and applications within a very short amount of time, similar to cramming for a test. Distributed practice, or *sustained reflection and recall,* over longer periods of time is the key to retention.

# PMI Thinking Strategy

Edward de Bono developed a clever strategy to analyze the positive aspects (P–Plus), the negative aspects (M–Minus), and the interesting aspects (I–Interesting) of an issue. In this variation, I also add a graphic to represent the issue or problem being discussed. (See de Bono's websites for more ideas and information: www.debonogroup.com; www.edwdebono.com; www.sixhats.com.)

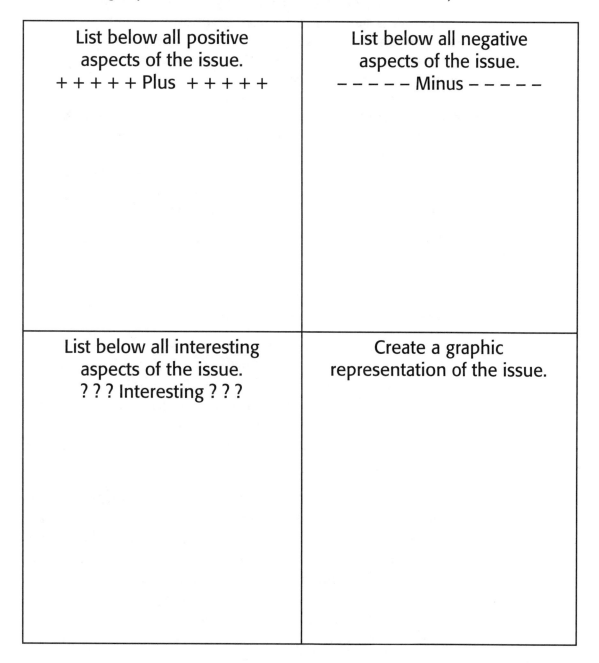

| List below all positive aspects of the issue. + + + + + Plus + + + + + | List below all negative aspects of the issue. – – – – – Minus – – – – – |
|---|---|
| List below all interesting aspects of the issue. ? ? ? Interesting ? ? ? | Create a graphic representation of the issue. |

## DISTRIBUTED PRACTICE AND SPIRAL CURRICULUM

Reflection activities shouldn't be limited to just the first or second lessons. Nearly 30 years ago, Madeline Hunter described *distributed practice* as practice and recall activities that are distributed over long periods of time. Providing review of critical skills and key points at regular intervals throughout the year helps with retention. Teachers should try to create connections to prior learning that emphasize its importance to students.

Many curriculum programs have built in a *spiral curriculum* through which earlier skills are reviewed periodically. Spiral models have merit based on brain research, but only if the initial concept was actually learned in an experiential way and had reflection opportunities immediately following. Otherwise, as the skills and concepts are rotated back into the course, the learners are routinely reminded of what they never really learned to begin with!

# Orchestrate Frequent Opportunities for Choice

Not only do teachers need to have various process activities ready to go, the activities must have some flexibility. Adjusting activities to meet learners' individual readiness levels will be key. A clever sense-making activity will be meaningful only if the learner didn't already know the concept. Be ready to adjust the activity to be more complex or more basic as the need arises.

As we make sure that all students are gaining understanding of a particular skill or concept, our tendency is to accelerate those students who have already demonstrated a basic level of competency. *Give the student the next harder concept.* This is how standard gifted programs have often operated. Parents even insist that a student "already did this kind of math *last* year," or "at home reads much more difficult books," or they ask, "Please send home harder assignments for homework."

## Lateral Enrichment and Expansion

More than 20 years ago, I attended a workshop by Roger Taylor, an expert on teaching gifted students, and he showed a diagram similar to the one below. He emphasized the importance of striking a balance between acceleration and lateral enrichment or expansion. When students begin to understand, it isn't always necessary to move them ahead on a continuum. Enrichment and expansion projects that will have students apply and transfer their new knowledge to a different situation are invaluable. Expanding the initial understanding by synthesizing and creating new variations can enhance learning.

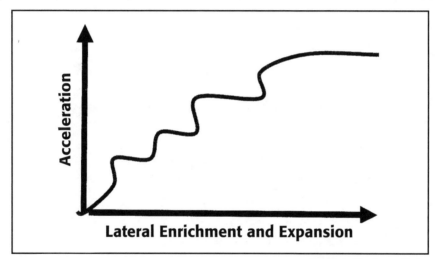

Suggested by Roger Taylor

For teachers trying to differentiate instruction, this model is extremely useful. Rather than differentiating by always accelerating the more capable student, provide enrichment and expansion of a topic. That way, at the end of a unit or lesson, the gap between higher and lower achieving students in their understanding of basic concepts won't be a huge chasm. To the students, the activities will seem more related, and they will often notice the different levels of understanding within the class.

# Teacher down the Hall Story

I once taught a group of intermediate students about early time-keeping devices. I had briefly introduced the Greek *clepsydra,* a water clock. In cooperative learning groups, the students were to create a type of water clock using a large Styrofoam cup with a hole punctured near the bottom. Using measuring cups and stopwatches, they were to try to create a device that measured one minute. (They could alter the size of the hole or the amount of water until it worked.) Many students were just playing with the materials; my guess is that most were lacking in experiences with basic water play. As they went through several cups and a lot of water, some students got the idea and were ready to go. I gathered these students together in a new group. For them, I *expanded* the original task to include some of the following questions and activities:

- How accurate was their clepsydra? With at least 10 trials, what was the variation in time, using the same amount of water?
- Could they predict the amount of water they would need to have a clepsydra that measured 30 seconds? Two minutes? Three minutes?
- What variables hadn't they originally considered?
- How might using sand or salt instead of water affect the results?
- Using the resource books available in the library, find out the circumstances in which the Greeks used clepsydras.
- Did any other cultures invent water clocks?

## Tiered Groups

The example of the water-clock builders (in the box opposite) shows how you can create tiered groups to provide at lease two levels of complexity for the same topic. One group continued with the basic challenge, and the other group, identified by a quick observational assessment, were asked to extend their own learning. Some worked on their own; others preferred to stay with a partner or in small groups.

Chapter 6 explains how curricular content can be tiered based on levels of complexity. You can use tiered assignments to differentiate instruction in multiple ways. Diane Heacox, in her book *Differentiating Instruction in the Regular Classroom* (2002), describes six ways that you can use tiered activities to reach and teach all learners.

- ◆ Tier by challenge level.
- ◆ Tier by complexity.
- ◆ Tier by resources.
- ◆ Tier by outcomes.
- ◆ Tier by process.
- ◆ Tier by product.

Tiered assignments can be more complex and detailed for advanced students and may, at first glance, appear to take more time and be longer. The rule of thumb is to anticipate how long the activity would take based on the abilities of the learners. A frank discussion about differentiation must take place to explain these differences in assignments to students (see page 139).

> Tiered assignments are differentiated learning tasks and projects that you develop based on your diagnosis of students' needs. When you use tiered assignments with flexible instructional groups, you are prescribing particular assignments to particular groups of students. Within each group you decide whether students do the task alone, with a partner, or as a collaborative team.
>
> —Diane Heacox (2002, 91)

**TIERED ASSIGNMENTS WITH IDENTIFIED GROUPS**

| Blue | = | struggling readers and writers | least complex activities |
| Red | = | competent readers and writers | more complex activities |
| Green | = | independent, advanced readers and writers | most complex activities |

*Note: Tiered assignments for the groups are purposefully* not *listed as "lowest" first.*

# Newspaper Search Tiered Assignment Example

Use the classroom copies of the *San Jose Mercury News* to respond to the following tasks. Read the directions carefully. Write answers on a separate sheet of paper. Use complete sentences. When you are finished, meet with your group to check your answers. Be prepared to share with the rest of the class what you find.

**All students:** On the front and back pages of the front section, read "Woman Who Swam from Cuba to Florida." Search the article for facts that include *numbers* in them. Write a good complete *declarative* sentence for each fact. Use lined paper and super-neat handwriting. Blue = three facts; red = four facts; green = five facts.

*In addition, groups should do the following tasks.*

**Red group:** Read the article "Coffee Price Rise Trickles" on the front page of the C section. Be sure to read the end of the article on the back page. Write your responses neatly, in complete sentences, on your lined paper.

1. Describe reasons why coffee prices are going up.
2. Discuss in a few sentences what some companies, like Starbucks, are going to do.
3. Predict what coffee drinkers will do if the price goes up.

**Green group:** Read the article "Nasal Flu Spray" on page 2 of the F section. Write your responses neatly on lined paper.

1. Analyze and discuss some hurdles that the manufacturers of the flu spray had to overcome.
2. Pretend it is the year 2020. Write a summary of changes and what great or terrible things have occurred for the population since the introduction of the flu spray.

**Blue group:** Read the article "Surgeons Reattach Boy's Arm" on page 3 of the B section. Answer these questions in complete sentences on your lined paper.

1. Describe how the boy's arm was ripped off.
2. Tell what the doctors did.
3. Explain what the doctors think about his recovery.

# Novel Study Tiered Assignment Example

Respond to the following inquiries about *The Big Wave,* by Pearl S. Buck, on another piece of paper.

- Use complete sentences.
- Think about your answers.
- Check your spelling.
- Use neat handwriting.
- Organize your paper with care.

**All students:** Illustrate a favorite scene from the story. Include details and color.

**Red group:**
1. Describe how Jiya acted after the disaster. Explain how you think you might have acted.
2. Analyze the ways Kino's family helped Jiya deal with his grief. Evaluate whether they could have done anything else to help.
3. Decide whether you liked the book. Write a brief book review for the library.

**Blue group:**
1. Describe the disaster that happened in the story.
2. Explain why you think Jiya made the decision that he did.
3. Decide whether you liked the book. Explain why or why not.

**Green group:**
1. Compare Jiya and Kino. Describe their similarities and their differences.
2. Write a brief epilogue to the story. Predict what you think happened to Jiya and his wife.
3. Describe whether you liked the book. Research and write a brief description of the author's background.

## Multiple Intelligence Preferences

When creating various activities, address a wide range of intelligences (see page 20) and higher-order thinking skills (see Bloom's Taxonomy on page 120). When encouraging and helping students process new information, provide tasks that allow them to work using their preferred learning styles and intelligences. In many of today's classrooms, students spend a majority of the learning time using only two or three of the intelligences: verbal-linguistic, logical-mathematical, and intrapersonal (readin', 'ritin' and 'rithmatic—done independently!). Students who have developed those intelligences will do well in school and will be seen as academically successful. We will see them later as the valedictorians.

But for students who have yet to develop those reading, writing, and math skills, we must provide a way for them to process the new information in ways that they learn best. When a challenging skill comes along, especially, see if you can have each student do an activity using his or her preferred intelligence, one that is already well developed, to process the new skill. Guiding students to draw, act out, or make up a rhyme or song might hook their interest and motivate them to take some time to process the new information or skill. We need to change our bait based on intelligences too!

When I am preparing process activities, I use the reflection questions on the opposite page to ensure that I don't forget any of the intelligences and that I prompt myself to develop a wide range of tasks. It is not uncommon for teachers to create many tasks that involve our own personal favorite and well-developed intelligence. Likewise, we may neglect or avoid designing tasks that we personally don't care for or actually don't even understand ourselves! I often create activities that involve making up a skit, role-playing, giving a computer slideshow presentation or an oral report, making a video, and so on, and as I do, I'm thinking, "Oh, those all sound so fun and interesting! Why, who wouldn't want to do one of those?" I have always had difficulty creating good activities that involve intrapersonal skills. I don't like working quietly alone, and I

# Differentiating Instruction with Multiple Intelligences

## Logical-Mathematical

- How can I bring in numbers and calculations?
- How can I help students develop logical sequences and classifications?
- How can I illustrate systems and patterns?

## Visual-Spatial

- How can I use visual aids: videos, photos, graphics?
- How can I encourage illustrating, building, visualizing?
- How can I use metaphors and lively descriptions?

## Musical-Rhythmic

- How can I connect key points to a melody or rhythm?
- How can I use music or environmental sounds during class?
- How can I encourage students to create jingles, rhymes, songs?

## Bodily-Kinesthetic

- How can I involve the whole body in a learning experience?
- How can I encourage role-play, drama, movement?
- How can I connect key points to a movement or gesture?

REFLECTION QUESTIONS

## Verbal-Linguistic

- How can I use the written or spoken word?
- How can I build vocabulary?
- How can I encourage conversations and discussions?

## Intrapersonal

- How can I evoke personal feelings or memories from students?
- How can I orchestrate more time for quiet reflection activities?
- How can I encourage students to think for themselves and form opinions?

## Interpersonal

- How can I orchestrate peer sharing and cooperative learning groups?
- How can I provide opportunities to have conversations, discuss opinions, share ideas?
- How can I encourage the positive social skills of speaking and listening?

## Naturalist

- How can I make connections to the natural world around us?
- How can I use manipulatives from the environment and bring in real-world objects?
- How can I encourage more outdoor exploration and work time?

used to project that onto my students. Make sure your own challenges and biases don't limit the range of activities you offer to your students.

*Reel Good Idea*

> **MATH FACTS MASTERY**
>
> When helping students master the multiplication and division math facts, I use a grid to generate a list of strategies that cover the multiple intelligences. I refer to the grid, opposite, often and implement new strategies to help students master the facts. I have also used this to create a Math Facts Demons Week. For most of each day during a designated week, I create an opportunity for students to master their own personal math demons—the facts they keep forgetting and haven't mastered to a level of automaticity. By using the various strategies—such as cartooning, music, beads, and movement games—I have had great success with students mastering those last few demons.

## The Choice Challenge

One of the most challenging strategies classroom teachers must regularly try to orchestrate is the opportunity for students to have choice. I believe that a key aspect of differentiating instruction is to have students frequently *choose* how they will process new learning. Allowing students to have some power to choose the type of activity, the degree of complexity, whether they will work individually or with others, and perhaps even *what* they will learn demands that we have some organizational systems in place (see pages 133–35). Choice is very brain compatible!

> *When we see a choice, our brain chemistry changes. Research indicates that when learners look forward to doing an activity and feel as if they have some control over the type of task, they feel positive and motivated. These feelings trigger the release of endorphins (neurotransmitters in the brain) that promote a general sense of well-being and confidence. Having choices allows the learner to feel more in control. Feeling in control of one's learning experience contributes to self-determination, self-confidence, and empowerment.* (Kaufeldt 1999, 141–142)

# MI Strategies for Mastering Math Fact Demons

Invite students to try some or all of these "intelligent" strategies.

## Verbal-Linguistic

- Recite the facts out loud.
- Write the facts out (e.g, "six times three equals eighteen").
- Make up story problems to illustrate a fact.

## Logical-Mathematical

- Organize a "Family of Facts" chart and look for patterns.
- Keep a record of your percentage correct each time you review the facts.
- Say the facts in order, starting with 1s.

## Visual-Spatial

- Illustrate each fact using a picture story.
- Create a cartoon for each numeral.
- String beads on a bracelet to represent a fact (e.g., three reds, three blues, and three greens = 3 x 3 = 9).

## Bodily-Kinesthetic

- Toss around the Multiplication Ball. Say the product for the fact your thumb is on.
- Organize a relay race. Each runner must complete two problems before returning to tag the next runner.
- Learn the trick for remembering the 9s math facts using your fingers.

## Musical-Rhythmic

- Chant the facts while keeping up a clever hand jive, tapping thighs, clapping hands, and snapping.
- Listen to and learn one "Fact Rock 'n Rap."
- Create a rhyme or song to help you remember one of *your* demons.

## Naturalist

- Illustrate a few of the facts using seeds, rocks, or seashells.
- Collect things from the garden to make a salad, using math facts as you gather and prepare. For example, two tomatoes cut into four segments = 2 x 4 = 8.
- Find someplace in nature where you might see a math fact represented.

## Intrapersonal

- Make new triangle flash cards for yourself.
- Play with the Multiplication Quizmo.
- Practice your facts with a multiplication computer game.

## Interpersonal

- Quiz a partner using flash cards.
- Play Buzz with the whole class. As the class counts around a circle, you must say "buzz" when any multiple of three (or other math fact) comes up.
- Teach the class how to remember a particular fact.

With the strong emphasis on curriculum standards, we have less flexibility in allowing students to determine *what* they will learn. However, teachers should be encouraged to orchestrate systems so that students can choose the *process* they would like to use to reflect on and extend their learning, as well as how they demonstrate understanding (see Chapter 8).

### Developing a System of Must Do's and May Do's

When allowing students choices in how they process new learning, I believe strongly in creating a balance of what parts of the activities are non-negotiable and what parts students could select for themselves. My dear teacher colleague Robert Ellingsen always called these *must do's* and *may do's.* This describes perfectly the system of some tasks being done by all students—required work, a non-negotiable—and some tasks being open to student selection based on their own interests. This is where lateral enrichment and expansion can be provided for all students, not just for the highly capable.

Although the terms *must do's* and *may do's* may seem more appropriate for primary students, I assure you that the concept is clear at any age. On occasion, with older students, I simply use the designation of *required by all assignments* and *choice activities.* Integrating choice into the process of *building* understanding will allow students to differentiate their own learning. This similar strategy can be used for culminating products that *demonstrate* understanding as well (see pages 116–119).

For example, when students study vocabulary or spelling words, *all* students must complete some basic tasks to study the words *and* they must choose from a list of additional tasks. Students love to point out the "you *must do* a MUST DO and you *must do* a MAY DO!" May do's aren't an opportunity for students to choose whether or not they want to do one. (See the example of a must do/may do project on pages 105–106.)

# Survival! Book Project

Name: _____

Book Title: _____ Pages: _____

Write the main character's name and describe his or her personality and motivation.

_____
_____
_____
_____
_____

Using complete sentences, describe the setting of the story.

_____
_____
_____
_____
_____

Using complete sentences, describe several parts where the main character had to demonstrate survival skills.

_____
_____
_____
_____
_____

Using complete sentences, describe a favorite scene in the story.

_____
_____
_____
_____
_____

Choose an activity to do from the list on the next page.

# Survival! Book Project Activities

All students choose at least *one* project from the list below. The Hugger Mugger group chooses at least *two* from the list. You may not choose one you have done before. Do your personal best. Use your "smarts" (multiple intelligences)!

▶ **Design** a new cover for your book. Include colorful details for the front and the back.

▶ **Compose** a well-written letter to a librarian telling why this book would be good to purchase for the library.

▶ **Illustrate** a detailed colorful poster that shows some characters or funny scenes from the story. Include the title.

▶ **Write** a one-page description of a possible video game using elements from the story.

▶ **Compose** a song (such as a rap) that tells the story line.

▶ **Write** a one-page new ending to the story.

▶ **Create** a mobile of the characters in the story.

▶ **Write** a description of one of the main characters of your story as if it is 20 years later. Tell what the character is doing now and describe what he or she is like.

*Teachers, Change Your Bait!* © 2005 Crown House Publishing Ltd. • www.CHPUS.com

**VOCABULARY STUDY (15 WORDS)**

**Must Do:**

- Use each of this week's words in a good, complete sentence, using neat handwriting.
- Choose any five words and look up the definition of each in our classroom dictionaries. Write down the definition, part of speech, and page number where you found the word.
- Choose five more words and write them down, breaking them up into syllables and placing the accent mark appropriately.

**May Do** (choose one):

- Create a crossword puzzle that uses at least six of the words. Use graph paper.
- Choose five words and draw a picture that represents the meaning of each.
- Find at least five words or their letters in magazines or newspapers; cut them out and glue them on paper.
- Alphabetize the words.

The part of the assignment that is non-negotiable is usually easier to evaluate and grade. It should have clear outcomes and expectations, and students should be aware how points will be assigned or how a grade will be determined. The choice activities do not always address exactly the same skills or tasks, so they may have to be assessed differently.

### Include Homework Choices for Processing

When I assign homework to students, I try to have some choice built in as well. There are always days when the homework will be to finish at home what they were working on in class. In K–8 classrooms, I like to send home a weekly sheet that outlines the additional assignments that are expected to be completed during that week. Many of the choice activities are difficult to assess for completion and effort, so they are encouraged and expected, but students do not face consequences if they don't complete them. (See the example homework sheet and reading log on pages 108 and 109.)

# Ms. K's Class

Name: _____

## Homework

Week of May 5, 2003

### Vocabulary and spelling:

Write down the words for the week. Take them home and study them for a pretest on Thursday.

### Reading:

Read each night for at least 20 minutes. Record the title of the book and pages read on the reading log. Have a parent initial the log.

### Invention and science fair:

Use this week to finish your invention *or* science fair project or display. Bring it in next Monday to school for the evening open house and fair.

### Life skill—responsibility:

Discuss this life skill with your parent(s). Find out some times when they have had to be particularly responsible. What are some things at home that you are responsible for?

### Homework choice activities:

Discuss the ideas listed here with your parent(s) and decide on and *do* at least *one* additional activity this week. Record what you did on the reading log and have your parent sign that you did it.

- Go grocery shopping with your parent and compare prices.
- Help cook a whole meal.
- Work in the garden.
- Watch a program on the History or Discovery Channel with your family.
- Fix something that is broken.
- Study math facts.
- Practice cursive by writing a letter.
- Practice some additional time on your instrument or at a sport.
- Make up a list of eight things that would be good to put on this list.
- Make up and do an activity with your parent.

# Reading Log

Name: _____  Due on: _____

| | Book Title | Pages (or minutes) | Parent Initials |
|---|---|---|---|
| Day 1: _____ | | | |
| Day 2: _____ | | | |
| Day 3: _____ | | | |
| Day 4: _____ | | | |

## Homework Choice

This week for my homework choice I did _____

_____

_____

_____

_____

_____

Parent Signature: _____

Parents have shown nothing but enthusiasm and relief when I give this type of choice homework. Many parents have thanked me for including the choice activities. The parents report that by having choice, students are much more likely to actually do homework, and it also gives parents a wide range of other types of activities they could provide for their children.

### Choice Centers for Processing

Primary classrooms are often organized around *rotation centers.* Three to five groups of children might be at stations doing separate tasks while the teacher works with a small group on guided reading. This pattern lends itself well to introducing opportunities for students to make choices. Creating a system for record keeping is essential. A clear set of procedures and time-management strategies will help center work go smoothly.

> *Schedule students for three or four center rotations, then allow them to choose their last one. Display the assignments for centers on a board with labeled clothespins, tongue depressors, or 3-by-5-inch cards in pockets. As students arrive in the morning, they check the center board, determine where they will begin that day, and select something they may do. They take their name stick or card and place it at the sign of the center they would like as their free choice. Limit the number of students in each choice center; the first four, for example, get to be in that center. (Kaufeldt 1999, 151)*

To facilitate the rotations for a week, some teachers print out schedules and distribute them on Monday morning. Students keep them in their learning logs or folders to refer to as they go to their "must do" stations.

# Use Available Technology Resources

When I first began teaching more than 25 years ago, the most exciting technology resources I could use in the school were the following:

- ◆ 16mm films checked out from the county library
- ◆ filmstrips—sometimes with sound
- ◆ reel-to-reel Wollensak tape recorder

- adding machine with a pull-down handle.
- single phone line to the school—in the office

Within five years, several items had worked their way into the classroom:

- Texas Instruments calculators (desktop—not pocket-sized yet)
- cassette tapes for a listening station and headsets for up to eight at a time
- overhead projectors (routinely used in the classroom)
- a large TV and a VCR on a rolling cart, available to each wing of the school (You had to sign up in advance to use it, and you had to have completed a VCR training course on how to use it.)
- intercoms and phone extensions in *some* classrooms

As a classroom teacher, I take for granted the technology available to me and my students now.

- TVs, VCRs, and DVD players installed in most classrooms
- desktop computers, laptops, and PDAs available for student use in many classrooms
- many classrooms wired with high-speed Internet connections (for students and for teachers, who can plan, prepare, keep records, and research lessons online, as well as post assignments on personal websites)
- homework help available for students via telephone or Internet
- classroom and school websites
- presentation programs such as HyperStudio, Power-Point, and Kid Pix, enabling students to create multi-media research presentations
- advanced overhead projectors that also project from books, computers, and so forth
- digital camcorders and cameras for student productions
- school TV studios for daily productions by students and for satellite links from the world.
- individual email addresses for students
- automated phone systems to call parents and students regarding absences, upcoming events, schedule changes, and so forth

Although many lament that some of the things on the above list are not yet available at their schools, many teachers are obviously not using the technology that is available. While designing various processing activities, don't forget to use (and don't avoid using) the technology that is ready for student use. Most students are already technology savvy. We are the ones who need to see daily opportunities to integrate computers, cameras, phones, and so forth into the tasks we assign to students.

Recently, at an Apple computer conference, it was mentioned that we should think of the students we serve as *technology natives,* that is, born into it—exposed from birth! Most adults who teach them are *technology immigrants*; we migrated to it over the last 20 years. We know other ways to do things and see today's technology as faster, more efficient, and more global than the old ways. We still know how to type on a manual typewriter and make carbon copies (Have you tried buying carbon paper lately?); we know how to boil water and cook without a microwave; we know how to go to the library and look things up in an encyclopedia or card catalog. Our students don't. They are ready and waiting for us immigrants to use technology as an integrated part of the learning process.

To maximize the new learning and connections that are made in the brain, educators must capitalize on and enhance the experience by orchestrating multiple processing activities. Changing the lures and bait several times is not always just to hook learners into having an "aha!" moment. Sometimes we spend a lot of time organizing the initial activity only to discover that the students retained very little. By using diverse strategies that include *choices* for active processing, we can deliberately assist students in benefiting from and making sense of the experiences. The multiple intelligences can become a helpful tool when designing a variety of processing activities. Guiding students to *reflect* on what they have experienced or discovered will strengthen their capacity to retain the new information.

**PROCESSING NEW KNOWLEDGE WITH TECHNOLOGY**

Integrate opportunities for students to

- use the telephone at home or from class to research information
- share information with the class using the overhead projector
- make a computer slide show presentation (such as PowerPoint or ShowReal) to explain or demonstrate something
- use a digital camera to take pictures of a project or to research something outside the classroom
- produce a video with sound about a topic they are studying
- videotape other students while interviewing them about their opinions on a topic
- gather and play music clips that illustrate what they are studying
- at home, record a commercial and show it in class, describing the persuasive advertising techniques being used
- use clip art to illustrate a story or report created in a word-processing program
- compose and record a song, jingle, or melody to help them remember what they are studying
- use a timer on the overhead projector (such as the TeachTimer available at kaganonline.com) to help them keep track of work time
- use a noise monitor (such as the stoplight monitor that indicates noise levels with a red light, yellow light, and green light, also available at Kaganonline) to help them monitor their own noise levels
- hear instructions, discussions, and so forth through an auditory enhancement system with speakers in four corners and a wireless microphone for you (see www.audioenhancement.com)
- use a laser pointer to highlight slides and overheads

### *Tackle Box Ideas*

♦ Have students supply a spiral notebook and begin a reflection journal. Orchestrate times during lessons for them to write down thoughts, opinions, questions, and ideas.

♦ Create a task that involves tiered assignments. Orchestrate three degrees of complexity for students to complete. Assign the students to the tasks or arrange the tasks as a choice activity.

♦ Design one activity per week that has a "must do" and a "may do" component.

♦ Develop a greater understanding of MI. Use the planning questions to ensure you address each of the eight ways of processing information every week.

# 8
# Varying the Products
*Building and Demonstrating Understanding*

▶ Orchestrate meaningful culminating projects for students to apply their understanding through authentic achievements.

▶ Build higher-level tasks, inquiries, and activities using Bloom's taxonomy.

▶ Design various products and performances for students to demonstrate their understanding using their multiple intelligences.

*A product is a vehicle through which a student shows (and extends) what he or she has come to understand and can do as a result of a considerable segment of learning.* (Tomlinson 1999, 43)

The various elements of differentiated instruction and curriculum are difficult to single out, because in practice, they should be tightly woven together. This integrated approach to orchestrating content, grouping, environment, presentation, process, and products, when done well, should appear as simply a *powerful learning experience* to the students. Chapter 7 focuses on the importance of varying students' processing strategies to enable them to build their understanding of the concepts. This chapter investigates possible products and performances that enable students to demonstrate their understanding of skills and concepts.

# Orchestrate Meaningful Culminating Projects

Well-designed products and performances can help students build understanding. They can and should be *assessed* (not just evaluated or graded), and feedback should be given to the student by a peer, a parent, or the teacher. The most powerful feedback should be from the student, as part of self-reflection and self-assessment based on agreed criteria. This processing and product-making practice will prepare students for a culminating project that will enable them to demonstrate their understanding through an authentic assessment, as described in the next section of this chapter. (See more about ongoing assessment and feedback, as well as the distinction between evaluating or grading and assessing, in chapter 10.)

## Show What They Know

At the end of a unit, and after having many opportunities to develop their understanding, students are ready to show what they know. Patt Walsh, a colleague of mine many years ago, referred to this task as R. M.—it *really matters*. A test or quiz could be an R. M. experience; those scores and results could certainly affect one's grade. But test scores often don't tell the student, teacher, and parents what the student has really learned and whether he or she can put the new knowledge into use when needed in real life.

> **AUTHENTIC ACHIEVEMENT**
>
> A key element of the school-restructuring movement of the 1990s was the emphasis on *authentic learning,* in which students are engaged in substantive conversations, exploration, and inquiry designed for how the brain learns naturally. To assess their understanding, culminating products and performances must also be significant, worthwhile, and meaningful. Newmann and Wehlage (1993) suggest designing tasks to emphasize three criteria:
>
> - Students construct meaning and produce knowledge.
> - Students use disciplined inquiry and processing to construct meaning.
> - Students aim their work toward production of discourse, products, and performances that have value or meaning beyond success in school.

Fred M. Newmann, author of *Authentic Achievement* (1996) and former director of the Center on Organization and Restructuring Schools (CORS) at the University of Wisconsin, has been a strong advocate for authentic teaching, learning, and assessment practices in schools. Educators who believe in *authentic learning* believe that the most accurate way to see what a student knows is for the student to create a genuine, real-world product. Authentic learning enables students to explore, discover, discuss, and meaningfully construct concepts and relationships in contexts that involve real-world problems and projects that are relevant and interesting to the learner (Donovan, Bransford, and Pellegrino 1999). This kind of achievement is significant and meaningful as opposed to tests and traditional forms of assessments that rely on efficient, simplistic tasks and often focus on trivial and useless information.

Educators implementing brain-compatible teaching and learning strategies also believe that alternative assessments (that focus on authentic achievements) can best determine what

> Authentic achievement involves *producing* knowledge rather than *reproducing* it.
>
> —Fred M. Newmann (1991)

students really know. Teachers feel pressure to implement traditionally formatted tests from textbook programs and to administer yearly standardized tests, but they usually discover more of what a student has learned, and *not* learned, as a result of a real-world culminating project. Student motivation and interest are also increased when they are encouraged to put it all together and are ready to demonstrate their recent learning through an *authentic achievement.*

Design culminating projects first; that is, plan with the end in mind. Deciding on the type of real-world tasks that a student should be able to demonstrate at the end of the unit will guide lesson design, instruction, and curriculum mapping. Investigate the skills and concepts to be learned and determine in what context one would observe these things in a real-life setting. An artful educator will use this opportunity to implement integration of different subjects (see Integrated and Interdisciplinary Curriculum on page 68).

Investigate possibilities in the following three major project categories:

| **PUBLICATIONS** |  **ART AND SCIENCE REPRESENTATIONS** |  **SIMULATIONS, SERVICES, AND PERFORMANCES** |
| --- | --- | --- |
| • Books<br>• Newspapers<br>• Brochures<br>• Posters<br>• Website design<br>• Plays<br>• Advertisements | • Paintings or murals<br>• Models<br>• Sculptures<br>• Blueprints and designs<br>• Constructions using various materials<br>• Inventions | • Mock trials or debates<br>• Role-play and simulation<br>• Museums and exhibits<br>• Community service<br>• Video productions<br>• Fairs and festivals |

### Individual or Group Product?

Whether the task will be completed by individual students or by small groups is another consideration in selecting possible culminating projects. Individual products are easier to evaluate to determine what each student knows. Group products have to be cleverly designed to ensure that each student has a part to complete that will allow him or her to demonstrate understanding for an evaluation.

### Assigned Task or Student Choice?

When deciding on a product or performance that will be evaluated, I usually don't allow many choices. The structure of a task could be the same for everyone, but the content they choose to develop within the structure could be individualized. I often use the same "must do" and "may do" strategy as described on page 104. Even when part of a group, students should have some elements of the project be their own personal responsibility to complete in order to show what they know.

### Limiting and Guiding Choices

When allowing students to choose their own culminating project, I often will guide them to particular inquiries or tasks. This may be because I know what their readiness skills are or that I'm concerned that they may not have the necessary resources available to complete a certain task successfully. I may even limit their choices, based on past efforts or selections. If a student has been selecting the same type of product to demonstrate understanding, then I may say that, for this project, he or she must choose between two or three other types of products to extend the student's experience and build his or her strengths using other intelligences.

## Build Higher-Level Tasks, Inquiries, and Activities Using Bloom's Taxonomy

About 50 years ago, educational psychologist Benjamin Bloom edited and published a framework for categorizing educational objectives: *Taxonomy of Educational Objectives* (1956). Its original purpose was to create a classification of student learning outcomes that could help professors create better questions on tests. "A taxonomy is a special kind of framework. In a taxonomy the categories lie along a continuum" (Anderson and Krathwohl 2001, 4). *Bloom's taxonomy,* as it is usually called, is a set of six categories of ways to think about things, arranged in a hierarchy from least demanding to most demanding.

## BLOOM'S TAXONOMY OF THE COGNITIVE DOMAIN
(lowest to highest levels)

| Category | Cognitive Process | Process Verbs |
|---|---|---|
| **Knowledge** | Retrieve relevant information from long-term memory. | Recognize, recall, tell, define, repeat, list, label, recite, memorize |
| **Comprehension** | Construct meaning from oral, written, and graphic communications. | Explain, interpret, summarize, rewrite, describe, paraphrase |
| **Application** | Carry out or use the information in a given situation. | Implement, construct, demonstrate, operate, use, illustrate, translate |
| **Analysis** | Break material into parts and determine how parts are related. | Organize, compare, classify, differentiate, categorize, critique |
| **Evaluation** | Make judgments based on criteria and standards. | Judge, rate, prioritize, estimate, choose, conclude, justify, rank |
| **Synthesis** | Put unrelated elements together to form a new pattern or structure. | Produce, create, invent, compose, design, generate |

I first became familiar with Bloom's taxonomy as a teacher and curriculum developer for a gifted and talented (GT) program in the early 1980s. As I designed tasks and projects for these high achievers and highly capable students, my goal was to select and emphasize objectives from the highest three levels of thinking. It was widely believed then, as it is now, that the majority of regular classroom work is focused on the lowest levels of thinking. All students are capable of thinking and processing at the higher levels, but GT programs emphasize frequent experiences with projects and tasks that require higher-order thinking (HOT) skills.

As described by Newmann, authentic learning tasks should require students to use HOT skills. When students are required to use only lower-order thinking (LOT), they are usually the victims of "spray and pray" teaching and are just reciting and retelling information, doing lots of routine, repetitive practice. At the other end of the continuum, there are classrooms where almost all students are performing HOT most of the time.

---

### INQUIRY METHOD

In my early days of teaching, I used social studies and science programs that emphasized the inquiry method, or approach. The significance of designing tasks and activities using the inquiry method was twofold.

One advantage was that now the assignment was not easily turned into a simple question that could be answered in single-word responses. Instead of "Where did the battle take place?" (Answer: <u>Lexington</u>), the inquiry would be stated as *"Describe,* in a short paragraph, the location of the battle. Include location, terrain, proximity to a town, and the weather that day." The task demanded thinking and an elaborated response.

The second advantage is that when each task began with a process verb (see page 120), students could easily see what kind of task the inquiry was demanding. Both the multiple intelligences to be emphasized and the level of thinking to be used could be determined by quickly looking at the process verb. This made choosing between several different inquiries much more efficient.

**SIMPLE SYSTEM FOR DESIGNING GOOD INQUIRIES**

A good inquiry product can be developed using a simple formula:

content + process + authentic tasks + multiple intelligences + assessment criteria = good product

- **Content:** Identify the curriculum standards, skills, and concepts in which you want the student to demonstrate competency through a product or performance.
- **Process:** Select a process verb or verbs from a level of thinking that you want students to use. Start the inquiry with the verb to create an imperative statement (a command). This helps you avoid posing questions that generate yes or no responses.
- **Authentic tasks:** Design a complex authentic task that integrates a wide range of the skills, concepts, and standards, and, if possible, various curriculum areas.
- **Multiple intelligences:** Review the inquiry to identify which of the "eight kinds of smart" will be most used by the student to complete the task (see a summary of the intelligences on page 129).
- **Assessment:** Develop appropriate criteria for the final product. Include expectations regarding quality, quantity, and completion date.

Students use facts and skills to synthesize, hypothesize, interpret data, and draw conclusions. By using higher levels of thinking, students try to solve problems, discover new meanings, and demonstrate deep knowledge of a topic as opposed to achieving only superficial understanding.

Teachers often do not have much curriculum-development experience, yet we are for all purposes curriculum implementers. As we look for ways to differentiate instruction, varying the levels of thinking will be an important challenge. Use the taxonomy to examine the tasks and products that you create for students. By referring to the process verbs, you can, at a glance, determine what levels of thinking a particular activity requires. If you are in a situation where you have the freedom to design new curriculum, using Bloom's taxonomy can help to broaden the scope of experiences you provide. By learning and using the taxonomy's process verbs, all teachers can become competent at critically reviewing the curriculum choices we make with and for our students.

# Example Inquiry Products for Authentic Assessment

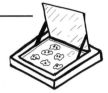

### SOLAR ENERGY UNIT (individual project)

**Construct** a solar oven using a medium-sized cardboard pizza box and aluminum foil.

- **Make sure** that it can be adjusted to maximize the reflection of the sun throughout the day.
- **Include** a window of clear plastic wrap to protect the food item to be cooked.
- **Describe** in a couple of written paragraphs how the oven works.
- **Decorate** the outside of your oven and give it a clever name.
- **Choose** a food item (such as quesadillas, cookies, apples, or potatoes) and cook it!
- **Write** a one-page description of your cooking experience and turn it in with the oven by April 1st.

### WESTWARD MOVEMENT UNIT WITH LETTER WRITING (individual project)

**Create** a book of correspondence: a collection of six letters exchanged between two people in the late 1800s. One lives on the East Coast and is well off. The other is a friend or relative traveling across the Plains in a wagon going to California.

- **Make** the letters interesting! Have the characters ask questions and describe what their lives are like.
- **Include** at least three references to things going on in the United States during that time period. For example, who was president? Had something been invented recently? Was there a war going on?
- **Mention** real towns and forts that are on the trail west as well as real places on the East Coast.
- **Keep track** of dates correctly. Remember how long it would take for mail to be delivered.
- **Create** an envelope for each letter. Include an East Coast return address, a postmark, and a mailing address. It is OK to use "c/o General Delivery, Fort Bridger."
- **Assemble** the collection of letters and envelopes into a booklet. Use the class bookbinding machine or bind it yourself. Creatively decorate the cover.
- **Hand in** the completed book by October 30th. See me if you need help or materials.

---

**MEASUREMENT UNIT (small group project)**

**Create** a measurement learning center for younger elementary students.

**Choose** English linear measurement (inches, feet, yards), metric linear measurement (centimeters, meters), English liquid measurement (cups, quarts, gallons), or metric liquid measurement (milliliters, liters).

Your mini–learning station should include various activities and items:

- A colorful and creative display board.
- A chart of equivalent measurements (such as how many quarts equal a gallon).
- Pictures of the measuring tools and containers to be used. Use drawings or magazine pictures.
- A set of eight task cards of activities that students could do to build their understanding of measuring. Gather the necessary materials for the tasks. (Each student in each group completes two tasks.)
- Photocopies of a worksheet with at least eight practice problems. (Each student in the group solves two problems.)

Have the learning center ready by Friday to bring to your primary class. They will really use it! Create a minitest of four problems to give students after the groups complete the learning-center tasks to see if the students learned the measurements. (Each student in the group solves one problem.)

---

When designing culminating projects for students, anticipate what additional skills are needed to complete the product successfully. If you have created a complex project that involves using a computer, consider whether each student has the necessary computer skills to complete the project successfully. Consider also what resources are available to all students. A video production or project that needs construction may be a challenge for some students. These considerations are especially necessary when offering some choices for final products. Ask yourself, "Will most of my students have the skills and resources available to them to make this project a viable choice?"

# The Wind in the Willows

## Book Project                                            Due: March 21st

After reading the novel *The Wind in the Willows*, select and complete inquiry projects from the following list. Do your *personal best*. Assemble written inquiries with a decorated cover. Spelling, sentence structure, and comprehension are important and count! Copy written inquiries a second time to improve neatness and correct mistakes. Copies of the book may be checked out.

**Earth Group:**   Minimum of two projects, one written
**Sky Group:**     Minimum of three projects, one written
**Sea Group:**     Minimum of four projects, two written

## Inquiry Choices

**Describe** in a well-written paragraph how Mole meets Ratty at the beginning of the story.

**List** the four main characters and write a couple of sentences about each one, describing who they are.

**Sequence** on a timeline at least six things that happen to Toad from his prison escape to his arrival at Ratty's home. Be creative! Use symbols and pictures to decorate.

**Illustrate** each of the four main characters using information given in the book.

**Describe** in a well-written paragraph the hobbies or fads to which Toad was attracted.

**Dramatize** Toad's monologue on page 192 ("Ho, ho, what a clever toad I am!") for the class.

**Recite** Toad's "Conceited Song" (from pages 192–93) to the class.

**Illustrate** in a storyboard format (separate scenes, like a comic book) the series of events that took place in chapter 5, "Dulce Domum." Write a brief description under each of the scenes (at least four).

**Create** small clay figures of at least two of the main characters.

**Design** a diorama or triorama of *one* of the following scenes:
- the taking back of Toad Hall from the Wild Wooders
- the barge woman and Toad on the canal
- Toad's escape from prison
- the picnic Ratty and Mole had in chapter 2 (include Otter too!)

**Describe** in two well-written paragraphs Toad's clever escapes: from Toad Hall and from prison.

**Paint** a scene from the story using watercolors. Write a brief description at the bottom.

**Evaluate** whether or not you think Toad is a likable character. In a well-written paragraph, describe some of his faults and his gifts and tell your opinion.

**Make up an inquiry of your choice and submit it for approval.**

## Teach Kids about Higher-Order Thinking

One of the most amazing results of designing good activities and projects using HOT skills is that students start recognizing higher- and lower-level tasks. I've had students comment that they wanted something more challenging! I also teach students about the levels of thinking and encourage them to make proposals. I give them a copy of Bloom's Taxonomy for Students (see page 127). I also show older students how I use the Simple System for Designing Good Inquiries (page 122) so that they know what I will be looking for in their proposals.

## Teacher down the Hall Story

One year I had a particularly clever group of fifth- and sixth-grade students. They loved designing their own proposals. They often created tasks for each other to do. That year they created several independent book contracts with inquiries that I still use! Each student had his or her own copy of Bloom's and knew the formula for creating great tasks and inquiries.

In the fall of the next year, a student returned to my class to visit. She had gone on to the junior high for seventh grade. One of her first questions to me was, "Hey, Ms. K. Do you have any copies of that 'Bloom's for Kids' thing we had last year?" I told her of course I had some and had just recently taught this year's students about the levels of thinking. She asked if she could have an extra six copies to take with her.

I thought this was a fairly unusual request, and I asked why she wanted them. "I want to give them to my teachers at the junior high," she replied, "because they don't know about higher levels of thinking. They always have us work at knowledge and comprehension and it's soooo boring! They have us read a chapter and then do the questions at the end. We looked at the verbs in those questions in the book—did you know that they are almost always just at the lower levels?" From the mouths of babes.

# Bloom's Taxonomy for Students

Six levels of thinking and process verbs
for inquiries at each thinking level.

**Knowledge**—Do you know it? Check the facts!

▶ tell, define, list, name, memorize, label

**Comprehension**—Do you understand it? Know the meaning!

▶ describe, discuss, explain, retell, translate, reword

**Application**—Can you use it to do something else? Solve problems!

▶ apply, dramatize, illustrate, interview, build

**Analysis**—Can you break it down into parts? Examine it!

▶ inspect, analyze, compare, classify, dissect, examine

**Evaluation**—Can you make a judgment? Make a decision!

▶ decide, judge, recommend, grade, evaluate, rate

**Synthesis**—Can you create or invent something new? Be creative!

▶ compose, invent, create, design, build, construct

Adapted from Anderson and Krathwohl 2001.

# Design Various Products and Performances Using Multiple Intelligences

When deciding on authentic products for students to demonstrate learning, consider MI. It may be possible for students to show what they know using one of their more developed intelligences. A student may be able to role-play a famous person giving a speech, for example, more easily than writing an essay on the same topic. Making a working model of an electric circuit might be a better way to demonstrate understanding than copying an illustration from the textbook.

> If we want students to realize their full intellectual potential, we must integrate activities that systematically develop the capacities of each intelligence in and through the academic curriculum, and we must change the bias of current curriculum that values almost exclusively verbal-linguistic or logical-mathematical intelligence.
>
> —David Lazear (2000, 192)

As I design culminating projects, I try to have the task involve at least two to three different intelligences. This usually means it can be done individually or with a small group and that there will be an illustrating, creating, or performing aspect as well as a written segment. Of course, mastery of some skills and standards can only be demonstrated using a particular intelligence:

- Writing mechanics can't be just explained or acted out; one must know how to write!
- Being able to illustrate perspective in a drawing is a better way to show the skill than writing about it.
- To get a driver's license, one must take a written test and a practical driving test to show proficiency.

The Products and Performances Using the Multiple Intelligences chart (page 129) lists possible culminating products and performances categorized by the dominant intelligence that each demands. Remember that each of these products could also be used to build understanding through process (see Chapter 7).

# Products and Performances Using the Multiple Intelligences

| VERBAL-LINGUISTIC | LOGICAL-MATHEMATICAL | VISUAL-SPATIAL | BODILY-KINESTHETIC |
|---|---|---|---|
| • Write a poem.<br>• Write a book.<br>• Give a speech.<br>• Keep a journal.<br>• Write an essay.<br>• Write a letter to the editor of a newspaper.<br>• Conduct a phone or email survey of others' opinions. | • Make a diagram.<br>• Create a timeline.<br>• Design a flow chart.<br>• Calculate a total.<br>• Make a bar graph.<br>• Organize a checklist. | • Illustrate the topic.<br>• Build a model.<br>• Take and display photographs.<br>• Design a comic book.<br>• Create a diorama.<br>• Make a poster or brochure. | • Dramatize the event.<br>• Conduct an experiment.<br>• Role-play a character.<br>• Describe what happened through interpretive dance.<br>• Create a human tableau.<br>• Construct a prototype. |
| MUSICAL-RHYTHMIC | NATURALIST | INTERPERSONAL | INTRAPERSONAL |
| • Compose a song, such as a rap.<br>• Create a jingle or rhyme.<br>• Compose the musical score to a video or slide show.<br>• Record sounds or interviews with people related to the topic.<br>• Make up a hand jive and chant to remember a key point. | • Display a collection you have made.<br>• Write a brochure about traveling to another country.<br>• Classify objects found in a location.<br>• Visit a location over time and report your observations.<br>• Look for patterns in weather, geology, and the environment and make predictions. | • Participate in a roundtable discussion or debate.<br>• Survey others for their opinions.<br>• Conduct interviews about others' experiences.<br>• Choose others to work with collaboratively. | • Assess your own participation and effort.<br>• Write your opinion as an editorial on the topic.<br>• Keep a personal journal or log of events.<br>• Take time for reflection, then share your opinion in a speech. |

## Start with Fewer Choices to Avoid Stress

I have found that in the beginning, many students are not ready for a lot of choices for culminating projects. Older students especially will ask, "Which one should I do to get a higher grade?" Even if I have brainstormed a dozen great inquiries that use most of the eight intelligences, I will often give only two to four choices. Usually, one will be verbal-linguistic; one will be visual-spatial; and one will be bodily-kinesthetic. Students can easily decide which of these few choices they want to do. Occasionally the entire task is assigned to all students—that is, no choices—but within the context of the task will be many opportunities for students to make personal choices about investigations, time management, and how to complete the activity.

Planning backwards often helps me design meaningful, multidynamic culminating products. Try to design projects, presentations, simulations, and special events that will not only incorporate the *content* of the curriculum, but also demand that the students use a variety of skills, thinking, planning, and problem solving. When you have come up with the ways in which you would like them to *demonstrate* their understanding, your curriculum planning and mapping are simplified. You can then take time to map out how you can help students go through a learning journey and arrive at the intended destination.

## *Tackle Box Ideas*

♦ Start the unit with the end in mind. Design an authentic learning task as a culminating project. Use this project as at least part of the student's evaluation.

♦ Design inquiry tasks using Bloom's taxonomy. Make sure several tasks are at the highest levels: evaluation and synthesis.

♦ Create a complex culminating product or performance that integrates at least two of the multiple intelligences.

# 9
# Managing the Variables in a Differentiated Classroom

*Designing Systems and Procedures*

▶ Orchestrate effective systems and procedures to manage student behaviors and time.

▶ Build in creative anchor activities to direct and engage students during *ragged time*.

▶ Plan for acceleration, enrichment, and remediation for students.

*F*or many teachers, uncertainty about how to manage a differentiated classroom grows into a fear that stops them from attempting to provide instruction based on their students' varied interests and needs. . . . Although managing a differentiated classroom is not always easy, progress in that direction tends to make school a better fit for more students. It also tends to make teaching more satisfying and invigorating. (Tomlinson 2001, 32)

I believe the single biggest roadblock for teachers attempting to implement differentiated instructional strategies is classroom management and organization. Most educators understand that the underlying philosophy of the No Child Left Behind movement is that one size doesn't fit all. Effective teachers recognize that not only must they modify the instructional strategies to accommodate all students, they must also frequently have more than one task or activity going on in the classroom at the same time. The challenge of orchestrating two, three, or more activities to occur simultaneously can be overwhelming. Teachers who feel they barely have control over the class when everyone is doing the same thing at the same time are intimidated by the thought of possible chaos if students are supposed to be completing various tasks.

I have observed teachers trying to juggle three concurrent student activities: a reading circle, independent work, and choice time. I call this the three-ring circus—teachers are often unable to focus with the circle groups because students who are supposed to be working on other tasks are constantly distracting them. Teachers appear to be constantly putting out fires, jumping up and going to a student who is off-task, doesn't know what to do, or is disrupting others. Eventually, out of frustration and exhaustion, the teacher will choose to have everyone return to the seating arrangement and everyone do the *same* assignment at the *same* time. Because the management system failed, the instructional strategy fails.

The brain is a pattern-seeking instrument that seeks organization when faced with chaos (Hart 1999). When learner-centered organizational systems and procedures are established, students will be able to detect what to do on their own. A well-prepared teacher will have pre-established procedures for each activity in the classroom. In many cases, students should be involved in the creation of the routines. Most important, students should know what the system is for getting help and what to do if they are finished with a task before others.

All classrooms will have students of mixed abilities. The cognitive range continues to get broader and broader due to our diverse population and varied prior experiences. Plan for these inevitable differences. Your basic teaching strategies should already include a design for accommodating or modifying instruction for the struggling learners as well as expanding opportunities for your most capable students.

## Orchestrate Effective Systems and Procedures

*Well-designed procedures for various activities allow for several different activities to be going on at the same time, which is imperative if you are orchestrating multiage classrooms or learning environments that encourage choice, movement, centers, and so on. Procedures can also help ensure that transitions take place efficiently, with a minimum of wasted time and confusion.* (Kaufeldt, 1999, 51)

Often students don't know a procedure for an activity because there isn't one! Teachers often make assumptions that students *know* certain patterns for doing things. When a teacher asks students to clean up, the students may not have the same level of understanding as expected. Simply asking students to "hand in your work" may create momentary chaos of movement and talking. Having a simple pre-established pattern for handing in work eliminates the confusion of assumptions.

Many activities and daily tasks should have established procedures. Students should know the pattern of behaviors you expect for each of these situations:

- ◆ arrival to class
- ◆ seating arrangements
- ◆ collecting assignments or other materials
- ◆ passing out assignments or materials
- ◆ getting basic needs met: water, restrooms, movement
- ◆ independent work

- group work
- use of supplies and materials
- cleanup
- dismissal

> Activity procedures are the written specific social/behavioral expectations for the various activities that occur within every classroom and that will hold for every time the activity takes place. . . . Once agreed upon, classroom procedures clearly define and establish the social parameters for specific activities, distinct from directions, which establish the task-related parameters of a specific activity.
>
> —Patricia Sequeira Belvel and Maya Marcia Jordan (2003, 112)

Follow these guidelines for well-designed procedures:

- Phrase in positive terms; tell what should be done.
- Be succinct and clear to students.
- Include graphics, symbols, and color.
- Write as imperatives; use process verbs to start the statements (see page 120).
- Include expected behaviors that are observable.
- Involve students in formulating.
- Review (and post) prior to the activity.

Classrooms that have clearly defined procedures provide students with a sense of security. When procedures are practiced and used routinely, students know what the behavioral and social expectations are for each task. They are able to self-monitor and cooperatively assist and guide others during work periods.

Now when you are trying to manage the three-ring circus, each task will have its own set of procedures. Most important, establish two guidelines ("What to do if you're done" and "What to do if you need help") that are posted and implemented all the time. (See sample procedure charts on page 135.)

# Sample Procedure Charts

### WHEN YOU'RE DONE WITH YOUR WORK

- *Recheck* your work.
- Be willing to *help others.*
- Do an extra *choice* or *"may do" activity.*
- Select an *anchor activity* (see page 136).

### IF YOU NEED HELP

- *Ask three* before me.
- Find a *peer helper.*
- Put your name on the *help list.*
- Keep working on a part that you *can* do.

### TEACHER AND STUDENT PRESENTATIONS

- *Listen* and *watch.*
- *Stay* in your seat.
- *Raise your hand* to share.
- *Join in* when asked.

### SMALL-GROUP ACTIVITY

- *Sit* or *stand* (not both).
- *Stay* in your group's area.
- *Share* materials, ideas, and responsibilities.
- *Everyone* participates.

### WORKING INDEPENDENTLY

- *Decide* on your personal goal or task.
- *Collect* all materials needed.
- *Work* at your own seat or at the back table.
- *Do* intrapersonal work.
- *Ask* for help quietly.
- *Stick with it!*

### READING CIRCLES AND DISCUSSION GROUPS

- *Listen* for your group to be called.
- *Bring* necessary materials.
- *Sit* in any available seat.
- *Check* agenda and *read* until teacher joins you.

# Chapter 9

# Build in Creative Anchor Activities

As students are completing different tasks at different rates, there will inevitably be periods when you must orchestrate how students can continue, wait, or help others. This anticipated *ragged time* (Tomlinson 2001) during differentiated activities worries many teachers. Basic classroom management systems are the key to success. Procedures should be established beforehand that give students the guidelines for what to do during ragged times. These systems will create a brain-compatible atmosphere by providing a sense of predictability and assurance of what will happen next. When there is too much ambiguity, many students will have so much anticipatory anxiety about what they should do next that they might not be able to focus on the task at hand.

One way to resolve the ragged time dilemma is to make sure there is an activity or project that all students can continue working on if they are finished or waiting for a turn for a conference or use of a computer, and so forth. Tomlinson calls these *anchor activities*.

> Using specified activities to which students automatically move when they complete an assigned task is important both to maintaining a productive work environment and to ensuring wise use of everyone's time.
> —Carol Ann Tomlinson (2001, 35)

Anchor activities are *not* busywork or time killers. They are often complex, multidynamic tasks that involve various levels of research and skills. In my classroom they are often part of a final culminating product or performance. Many tasks make good anchor activities. In general, they should

- ◆ be self-directed
- ◆ include aspects that can be completed on an ongoing basis
- ◆ relate to the concepts and content to be learned
- ◆ not necessarily involve other students
- ◆ be engaging, meaningful tasks—not busywork or packets of worksheets
- ◆ be activities that everyone will have a chance to do, even if not yet finished with other work

# Teacher down the Hall Story

In my early years of teaching, I would spend hours each week running off copies of student worksheets and activities that I fondly called "enrichment packets." In my elementary classes, the packets would have a lot of seasonal games, word searches, puzzles, and coloring pages. In the middle school classes, the packets would have mindbender-type puzzles and Plexers, word games and math stumpers. In high school English, I would always have some creative-writing prompts or difficult crossword puzzles.

The purpose of the enrichment packets was to keep the fast workers busy while the others caught up. Consequently, the slow workers rarely got to work on the packets during class time. I had the right idea but not well-developed tasks for anchor activities.

I have often used the idea of a culminating project folder as a great anchor activity. For each unit that we are working on, the students keep a folder of the inquiries and tasks that are assigned. At the end of the study, the completed folder is turned in as part of the overall summative assessment. Besides the assigned inquiries that are a "must do," there are a variety of other "may do" tasks in the folder. Students often make elaborate covers, even using pop-up book "technology"—using additional illustrations and explanations from other sources. Some students may return to previously finished assignments and add to them or redo them.

Culminating project folders make great anchor activities and also serve as great products to use in a portfolio of student work. In the spring, I ask students to select one folder of which they are most proud to use at a parent-student conference. After discussing what was great about the project and what improvements could be made at another time, the folder is stored in the student's portfolio as a benchmark.

Anchor activities can also be tasks that most of the class might be doing while you work with one group in a conference or discussion. An anchor activity can become one of the rotation centers, if you have them (see page 110). The tasks are often so interesting and real that students can hardly wait to finish the assigned activity so that they might get to the anchor task.

In my class, the anchor activity is often working on part of a culminating project that students will use to demonstrate their understanding. It can also have some choices involved.

*Reel Good Idea*

---

### ANCHOR ACTIVITY SUGGESTIONS

- journal writing
- continued reading of a novel or related resource
- finishing up miscellaneous work
- rewriting a rough draft
- using the computer for further research or word processing
- creating a brochure about the topic
- making a children's book about the topic
- preparing and practicing for a presentation
- writing letters to get more information on a topic
- designing a poster for a bulletin board
- finding amazing facts in the resource books and posting them
- cutting pictures about the topic from magazines for a bulletin board
- choosing an additional related activity from a "may do" choice list

---

# Plan for Acceleration, Enrichment, and Remediation

Each student in our classrooms is a unique learner. Each brain has developed with an individualized recipe of experiences and a personalized genetic code. The one-size-fits-all approach often ends up fitting no one very well. Although we may begin a lesson or unit with our best lure, we must assume that other lures and strategies will inevitably be needed. *Plan* for this reality. In my opinion, all lessons must at least be considered ahead of time as *tiered* (see pages 76 and 97–99). Be a good *maestra* and orchestrate the lesson and activities beforehand. This is much more effective than being reactive throughout the lesson and having to make improvised adaptations.

Integrating differentiated instruction into daily lessons and activities takes some practice. As you prepare students to expect that they will not always be doing the same assignment as other students, make sure they know that your intention is not to assign *more* work to more capable students and vice versa. Sometimes students, especially older students, will complain about the more challenging or difficult tasks assigned to them. If they have been able to get outstanding grades without much effort, these "smart" kids often stomp their feet a bit at being put on the edge of their own personal learning curve.

Keep in mind how tiered tasks are introduced and managed from the student's point of view.

1. When presenting the tasks to students, be enthusiastic about all levels of the assignments. Avoid always starting with the most basic or novice task. Vary the order of tasks on contracts and assignment sheets.
2. Make sure that all variations and levels of the tasks demand that students use varied higher-level thinking skills (see page 120) and a range of intelligences (see page 129).
3. Choose tasks for the different levels or choices that are equally interesting, engaging, and motivating for students.
4. Make sure that the degree of work seems relatively compatible with the learner's abilities and that it seems *fair* to students. Although the task is different, will it take comparable time and effort to complete?
5. If all students are working on tiered activities at the same time, make sure the tasks are equally active. Students shouldn't have to sit quietly to complete an assignment while another group is laughing and moving around (as they create a poster and presentation, for example).

## Accommodations for Struggling Learners

- Incorporate the use of a graphic organizer.
- Include graphics, photos, or cartoons in any written directions.
- Create and post clear procedures.
- Integrate opportunities to do at least part of the work with a partner.
- Create simple key phrases that relate to the work and can be repeated:
  - division algorithm: "Divide, multiply, subtract, bring down."
  - getting help: "Ask three before me."
  - high-scope activities (centers): "Plan, do, review." (See more information at www.highscope.org.)
  - returned work: "Get it, check it, file it."
- Encourage the use of highlighting markers and Post-it notes.
- Make copies of pages from textbooks for students to write on and mark up.
- When giving multiple problems to solve or exercises to complete from a text or worksheet, have students cross out alternate problems to reduce the number of items.
- Use formats that allow students to express what they have learned in ways other than written language.
- Divide tasks up into chunks that can be handed in and checked off incrementally.
- Make sure resources are available in various levels, languages, and modalities.
- Work with the students to create a visual timeline of expected completion dates.

## Strategies for English-Language Learners

In addition to the suggestions listed for struggling learners, consider incorporating the following strategies:

- Speak more slowly than you normally would and use short sentences.
- Gesture and use facial expressions to exaggerate what you mean.

- Avoid idiomatic expressions, and be aware of your own regional dialect.
- Find various ways to reword complex statements.
- Post key English nouns and phrases with pictures to illustrate meanings.
- Through questioning, see if the new information can be linked to the student's prior experiences.
- Limit and guide choice activities for the ESL students based on the resources available in their native languages.

## Enrichment and Acceleration for Capable Learners

- Create tasks that help stretch an advanced learner on many different levels: research skills, complexity of a problem, range of solutions, transformation, higher-level thinking, and so forth.
- Encourage these students to conduct their own research, make up their own experiment, and seek out a mentor.
- Be willing to adjust the time frame of the task.
- Help coordinate opportunities to work with an expert, a more advanced student, or a mentor in the field.
- Stretch the content by having the student examine the topic across time periods or in different cultures.

## Access, Equity, and Excellence for All

*Educators often speak of equity as an issue with children of the former group [struggling learners] and excellence as an issue for the latter [advanced learners]. In truth, equity and excellence must be at the top of the agenda for all children.* (Tomlinson 1999, 21)

Classrooms have changed little in the last 100 years, but the students have changed a lot. Many classrooms have been required to include children with special needs. Classrooms all across the United States and Canada have students with diverse backgrounds and native languages. When educators decide to design curriculum and instructional strategies that address a wide range of capabilities and experiences, *all* students will benefit.

Well-designed differentiated instruction in classrooms that are well grounded in brain-compatible best practices will be responsive to all students. Orchestrating variation will benefit struggling students, advanced learners, and second-language learners. Differentiation addresses gender differences and learning styles and is culturally sensitive. All students deserve a teacher who has a well-stocked tackle box and will do anything to help them realize their unique potential.

When the procedures and expectations are clear, students are more likely to engage and, ultimately, learn. Empowering students to know what to do in a variety of situations, how to get help, and where to get information are valuable lessons to incorporate and emphasize. It is disappointing to see so many of our students suffering from learned helplessness. A well-managed classroom environment can teach them the skills they need to be self-reliant adults.

## *Tackle Box Ideas*

♦ Anticipate the need for pre-established, posted procedures for each of the main activities in the classroom.

♦ When differentiating instruction, plan for ragged time and have a set of procedures in place so that students know what to do.

♦ Create meaningful anchor activities for students to do when they have finished a task or are waiting for help.

♦ Anticipate that each lesson will need a wide range of complexity and difficulty. Build in strategies for struggling learners, advanced students, and ESL learners.

# 10
# Using Ongoing Assessment to Plan Instruction and Give Feedback

## *Helping Students Show What They Know*

▶ Use immediate, ongoing feedback for assessment and to guide instructional planning.

▶ Teach self-assessment and goal-setting strategies to students.

▶ Use multidynamic, learner-centered rubrics to give accurate feedback and help set goals.

*S*ome people use the terms assessment *and* evaluation *interchangeably, but they have different meanings. When we assess, we are gathering information about student learning that informs our teaching and helps students learn more. We may teach differently, based on what we find as we assess. When we evaluate, we decide whether or not students have learned what they needed to learn and how well they have learned it. Evaluation is a process of reviewing the evidence and determining its value.* (Davies 2000, 1)

To ensure that each student continues to get what he or she needs in order to be successful, teachers must frequently assess how the student approaches, tackles, and performs each activity. This aspect of instruction can overwhelm teachers, because it implies a potentially massive amount of documentation and record keeping. Yet, this assessment information is crucial in determining what steps need to be taken next by the student, as well as in guiding instructional planning.

## Use Immediate, Ongoing Feedback for Assessment and Planning

*In a differentiated classroom, assessment is ongoing and diagnostic. Its goal is to provide teachers day-to-day data on students' readiness for particular ideas and skills, their interests and their learning profile. . . . Assessment always has more to do with helping students grow than with cataloging their mistakes.* (Tomlinson 1999, 10)

A well-developed lesson should incorporate multiple opportunities for students to *build* their understanding. During this active learning period, avoid grading the tasks that students do and instead give accurate feedback—formally and informally—checking for progress at designated benchmarks. Students should still be held accountable for participating and processing, but the products that they create during this learning time are really practice products. When learners know that even their first attempts at producing and demonstrating knowledge will "count" and be graded, the risk is greater and they are likely to feel more anxiety about the resulting product. Creativity will be limited, desire and interest will be diminished, and the outcome will often be rushed when there is a grade or extrinsic reward at stake. *Grades are often interpreted by students as an extrinsic reward system rather than as a summative evaluation.*

It is common to use assessment strategies that focus on the *deficit* model: pointing out what the student doesn't know and can't do yet. What if instead the feedback to students informed them of what they already know and what they have learned?

Many of the suggestions for assessment given in this chapter are designed to give the students a chance to show what they know.

> A system of rewards and punishments can be selectively demotivating in the long term, particularly where others have control over the system. It reduces the desire as well as the capacity of learners to engage in original thought. . . . Rewards for specific outcomes encourage people to focus narrowly on a task, to do it as quickly as possible, ignore other information, and take few risks.
>
> —Renate Nummela Caine and Geoffrey Caine (1994, 77–78)

## Determining Readiness

*Readiness is not a synonym for ability; rather, it reflects what a student knows, understands, and can do today in light of what the teacher is planning to teach today.* (Tomlinson and Eidson 2003b, 3)

At the beginning of the year or semester, you will often assess readiness while you are creating each student's profile. Part of the information gathered should help you see which students are well prepared for the course of study and skills to be taught. As you introduce each new skill or concept, you may need to make additional readiness assessments. While keeping the standards in mind, plan work that is a little too difficult for students and then provide the experiences and support they need to succeed at the new level of challenge.

Try the following tools to determine readiness:

- ◆ student surveys (such as All about Me; see page 19)
- ◆ KWL (see page 147): "What do you *know*?" "What do you *want* to know?" and (at the end) "What did you *learn*?"
- ◆ observations of products and process ("kid watching")
- ◆ conversations (See Effective Questions on page 146.)
- ◆ information gathering through informal dialogue
- ◆ skills checklists (often available from reading and math specialists, resource teachers, and tutors; see also the Reading Strategies Checklist example on page 148)

- ◆ recommendations from previous teachers, specialists, and parents
- ◆ student choices:
  - What are this student's preferences?
  - When given a choice of activities, which tasks is the student willing to try?
  - Which intelligence(s) is a student most dependent on?

Reel Good Idea

---

**EFFECTIVE QUESTIONS**

- What are you doing? Tell me about it.
- How did you do that?
- How did you make that? Tell me step by step.
- Could you give an example of that?
- What alternatives are there?
- What reasons do you have for saying that?
- How do you know?
- Why did you find that interesting?
- What would you do differently next time?
- Is there a pattern to this?

---

Ongoing assessment is what good teachers do purposefully and often unconsciously. Taking mental notes about how students are approaching and completing tasks gives us information to guide the next steps and strategies needed for instruction. Orchestrating ways for students to get feedback along the way, either from the teacher or from self-assessment, ensures that they will have information to adapt their process and refine their skills and understanding.

As the brain builds an understanding and a pattern for how things work, it needs accurate feedback to strengthen the memory and connection. If there isn't any feedback or if the feedback is delayed, then the brain may believe that the pattern it is developing is appropriate, even though it may not be correct. *Without immediate feedback to keep the new learning on track, the brain may actually wire an incorrect pattern for doing something.*

# KWL Graphic Organizer for Reading

Name: _____ Date: _____

Reading Selection: _____

| K<br>What I Know | W<br>What I Want to Know | L<br>What I Learned |
| --- | --- | --- |
| | | |

| What I Think I Know | What I'm Reminded Of | What I Wonder About |
| --- | --- | --- |
| *Before Reading:*<br><br><br><br>*After Reading:* | *Before Reading:*<br><br><br><br>*After Reading:* | *Before Reading:*<br><br><br><br>*After Reading:* |

Skills Checklist Example

# Reading Strategies Checklist

Student Name: _____ Date: _____

_____ Expects reading to make sense. Views reading as meaningful, not just decoding. Reads for enjoyment or information.

_____ Draws on prior knowledge. Uses what is already known about a topic to process and gain further information.

_____ Makes reasonable predictions.

_____ Uses pictures for cues.

_____ Self-corrects consistently.

_____ Expects reading to "sound right." Understands basic English word order.

_____ Reads in chunks (phrases).

_____ Uses knowledge of letter-sound relationships (i.e., decoding).

_____ Reads different ways for different purposes. Can skim for information.

_____ Visualizes. Actively creates mental movies of settings, characters, and so forth.

In addition, constructive feedback shouldn't feel threatening, which can minimize learning; it should, in fact, make us feel cared for and encouraged.

> *Receiving specific information on how and why an error has occurred, coupled with instruction on how to correct the error, helps these students master skills more effectively. Kline and colleagues . . . found that this form of instruction, called "elaborated feedback," can significantly reduce the instructional time required for learning disabled students to master certain educational goals. They assert that without such feedback, these learners often practice incorrect responses thus delaying the mastery of targeted skills.* (Jensen and Dabney 2000, 176)

The principles of ongoing assessment are basic:

- Build up your tackle box with various strategies to gather information on student understanding and progress.
- Use this information to guide the planning of instruction.
- Provide students with accurate, elaborate, immediate feedback to ensure they don't practice incorrect responses.

## Informal Assessment Strategies

- Documentation of products and process

  Develop a simple system for assessing a student's progress with completing a task or creating a product, such as a three-point rubric:

  1. needs more time or help
  2. working and progressing
  3. competent—needs enrichment

- Anecdotal records (such as flip cards)

  When working with small groups, record anecdotal comments about each student's progress in a flip card folder (see page 151) to help you plan future instruction.

- Clipboard cruising with address labels

  Print out a page of address labels with students' names and the date (see example on page 152). Leave space on the label for brief notes. As you are cruising around the classroom, carry a clipboard with these labels and make observations of several students. At the end of the day, peel off each label and place it in the student's file folder. Try to make an observation of every student at least once a week.

- Work samples
- Student journals (Check students' response journals to see how they describe their experiences.)
- Progress charts
- Benchmark quizzes
- Homework assignments
- Student questioning strategies (see Effective Questions on page 146)

◆ Inventories (learning styles, skills checklists, lists of "things to include" in a task)
◆ Photos, videos, audiotapes (teacher created and student created)

## A Teacher down the Hall Story

I always have my camera at school. I take photos of students in action, doing presentations, at recess, on field trips, at centers, and so forth. These photos would be on display in the classroom as soon as I had the roll developed—which may have been weeks after the fact.

In the 1990s I got my first small digital camera. We began to take snapshots of students holding projects and inventions. They learned how to incorporate these photos into portfolios, Hyperstudio projects, autobiographies, and so forth. The camera could be attached to the computer and the pictures printed immediately and posted on bulletin boards or otherwise displayed.

As the costs have gone down and the availability has increased, digital cameras can now be an integral part of assessment and feedback for students. Have you become digital camera literate? I believe that a moderately priced digital camera is a key tool in every classroom.

- Become familiar with the functions and features. Play around with it!
- Discover how quickly you can download the pictures to a computer.
- Create digital portfolios for students and save the pictures for later use.
- Learn how to print out copies for display or to send home to parents.
- Train students to use the camera. Remember, there are no wasted film issues. If the photos aren't worth keeping, delete them immediately.
- Use the pictures to provide immediate feedback. (I've even taken pictures of students curled up with a book during silent reading. I wanted them to know how great it was that they were into the story and how impressed I was with their work.)

## MAKE A FLIP BOOK

1. Use three to five 8½" x 11" sheets of paper and one half sheet.
2. Arrange in staggered layers, so that each sheet rests on top of another sheet leaving a half-inch of the page beneath showing.
3. Fold to form a book, with the half sheet in the middle, and staple.
4. Add a student name to each edge.
5. Create a flip book for each group of students.

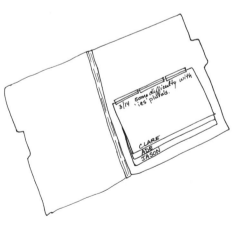

Use this flip book to keep anecdotal records of students in a small group for a short period of time. As you observe a new skill or an opportunity for reteaching, flip to that student's page and jot down a quick note. Date the entry if appropriate or use different colored pens on different days of the week.

## Variation:

## MAKE A FLIP CARD FOLDER

1. Use eight 5" x 7" index cards and a file folder.
2. Open the file folder and align one index card with the bottom edge of one side of the folder. Tape the top of the card in place.
3. Place the next index card on top of the first one but higher, so that a half-inch of the bottom card shows beneath. Tape the top of this card to the file folder.
4. Continue with the next six cards, staggering them to allow a half-inch of the card beneath to show and taping the top of the card to the file folder.
5. Add a student name to each edge (the half-inch of each card that shows).

# Clipboard Cruising Using Address Labels

| | | |
|---|---|---|
| May 12, 2005 Lynn A. | May 12, 2005 Emily A. *Finished six math tasks—Level 4.1. Should take unit test.* | May 12, 2005 Nick A. |
| May 12, 2005 Mike B. | May 12, 2005 Kyle B. | May 12, 2005 Ramesh B. |
| May 12, 2005 Ricki B. *Struggling with regrouping tens. Worked at back table with group.* | May 12, 2005 Keiko N. | May 12, 2005 Marie E. |
| May 12, 2005 Joli G. | May 12, 2005 Ray H. *Feeling successful today. Asked questions and stayed on task.* | May 12, 2005 Kurt K. *Feels confident. Says he knows it already! Keeps avoiding work.* |
| May 12, 2005 Kris K. | May 12, 2005 Mary M. | May 12, 2005 Shavoun M. |
| May 12, 2005 Julia N. | May 12, 2005 Miguel N. | May 12, 2005 Matt O. *Always singing and humming while working today.* |
| May 12, 2005 Brandy P. *Working well when sitting by Julia. Asks questions, gets help, and keeps going! Yea!* | May 12, 2005 Latisha R. | May 12, 2005 Sharron S. |
| May 12, 2005 Kyle T. | May 12, 2005 Adam T. | May 12, 2005 Greg V. |
| May 12, 2005 Cate W. | May 12, 2005 Hong Y. *Finished quickly. Asked to start on project work.* | May 12, 2005 Yasmin W. |
| May 12, 2005 | May 12, 2005 | May 12, 2005 |

# Teach Self-Assessment and Goal-Setting Strategies

*One big gift we can give kids is the gift of self-assessment, the ability to figure out for themselves how they are doing and what they need to work on. They don't learn this by being told "You're an 'A' math student." Or "Your behavior is poor." They need to learn how to monitor their own progress by asking themselves:*

- *Where am I at?*
- *Where am I going?*
- *What do I need to do to get there?*

*This type of self-assessment is very empowering. Instead of being something that's poured down you, education becomes something you figure out for yourself. If we teach kids how to think, not what to think, they develop strong values, and the confidence to make their own decisions later on in the face of peer pressure.* (Barbara Colorosa, quoted in Schwartz 1999, 33–34)

Providing frequent opportunities for students to show and demonstrate what they *do* know can build their confidence and self-esteem. Students gain confidence when they have a sense of control and mastery. As a student gains a sense of confidence in his or her abilities, self-esteem increases. Daniel Goleman, in his book *Emotional Intelligence* (1995, 95), says that "motivating ourselves to persist and try, try again in the face of setbacks" demonstrates powerful emotional strength.

When students can recognize and determine *for themselves* what they know, they develop feelings of competency and independence, as well as feelings of satisfaction when they see what they have accomplished. Sometimes students show surprise when they discover how much they already know! Waiting for someone else to grade, evaluate, or give feedback can encourage a feeling of helplessness and dependence.

Building self-esteem in our students has been a high priority for decades. In the 1960s the U.S. Department of Education conducted a $59 million educational research project called Follow Through. When all the data on various programs were reviewed, researchers found that the most influential models of instruction that contributed to raising students' self-esteem were those that focused on *competence* and emphasized *academic achievement*. By helping students be successful learners, we can raise self-esteem (Ellis 2001).

Being aware of the assessment criteria *before* beginning a task minimizes stress and confusion. If possible, include students in conversations before each learning activity. Discuss what the activity, project, or assignment will look like and what the expectations will be. Students will become more actively involved as the activity begins to take shape in their minds. They will begin to ask questions and develop motivation to start rather than experiencing anticipatory anxiety.

> As students participate in assessment, they learn to become partners in the continuous assessment cycle. In this cycle, students talk about what needs to be learned, set criteria, and receive and give themselves descriptive feedback.
>
> —Anne Davies (2000, 3)

Orchestrating time for student self-assessment and reflection helps learners integrate and consolidate new knowledge. When students have a chance to analyze what aspects of a concept or task have been learned, their brains reprocess the new learning and restimulate the new neural connections. The very act of self-assessment promotes the hardwiring of new learning in the brain. When they review what parts of a task were completed correctly and which were not, their brains create a pattern for what is correct and successful. This *shaping* of a new idea in their brains by matching and adjusting what works and what doesn't helps them form their mental model.

### METACOGNITION

*Metacognition* is the process of thinking about thinking. Learners who spend more time asking questions, analyzing, monitoring their own progress, assessing, and evaluating their learning process are generally more successful. When new learning opportunities arise, students with metacognitive experiences have a pattern of successful strategies from which to draw.

In addition there is a physiological reward to learning. Eric Jensen describes the evidence that when a cognitive task is completed, the brain produces an increased level of dopamine. This pleasure-chemical "reward" makes the learner feel good and even inspired to continue learning (Jensen 2003b).

## Self-Assessment Strategies

- quick self-check-ins: Fist to Five, Stalled or Cruising?, Thumbs Up! (see How Well Do I Know This? on page 156)
- project checklists (see the sample project checklist below)
- rubrics (including miniproject rubrics, such as on page 161)
- surveys (see Student Self-Assessment, on page 157)
- journals
- exit cards (Before students leave the classroom, tell them that they will each need to create and turn in an *exit card*, or a "ticket to leave." On this index card, they comment on or illustrate an aspect of the learning that just took place. Exit cards provide a quick way to assess student understanding.)

---

### "Into the Woods" Project Checklist

Name _____     Date _____

| **Date** | **Task/Activity** | **Comments** |
|---|---|---|
| _____ | Complete project turned in on time | _____ |
| _____ | Table of contents: neatly organized | _____ |
| _____ | Key questions: neat and complete | _____ |
| _____ | "What I Learned" essay, final draft | _____ |
| _____ | Cover colorfully decorated and neat | _____ |
| _____ | Activity/inquiry pages finished and organized | _____ |
| _____ | Inquiry project(s) (may do) completed | _____ |

Student signature: _____

Parent signature: _____

Teacher signature: _____

---

# How Well Do I Know This?

### Fist to Five

1 Finger Up  =  I'm just beginning and I'm confused.
2 Fingers Up  =  I'm starting to get it—a little.
3 Fingers Up  =  I need more practice and help.
4 Fingers Up  =  I'm doing pretty well on my own.
5 Fingers Up  =  I've got it! I could help others!

### Stalled or Cruising?
(spoken or prewritten on cards)

Stalled  =  I'm totally stuck and can't restart!
Minor Repairs  =  With some help, I can keep going.
Chugging Along  =  Safe speed. No problems
Cruising  =  Racing to completion!

### Thumbs Up!

Thumbs Down  =  I'm frustrated or lost.
Thumbs Up and Down  =  I'm in the middle.
Thumbs Up  =  I've got it!

*Teachers, Change Your Bait!* © 2005 Crown House Publishing Ltd. • www.CHPUS.com

# Student Self-Assessment

Name_____ Date _____ Subject: <u>Writing</u>

### Rate yourself along the scale for each of the following statements

| | | | |
|---|---|---|---|
| 1. I enjoy writing stories. | Never | Sometimes | Always |
| 2. I enjoy writing in a journal. | Never | Sometimes | Always |
| 3. I am good at spelling. | Never | Sometimes | Always |
| 4. I use a lot of descriptive words. | Never | Sometimes | Always |
| 5. I use the computer to write. | Never | Sometimes | Always |
| 6. I like to write long stories. | Never | Sometimes | Always |
| 7. My writing is mostly about real-life experiences. | Never | Sometimes | Always |
| 8. My stories are mostly from my own imagination. | Never | Sometimes | Always |

Finish each of the following statements:

My favorite topic to write about is _____

My least favorite thing about writing is _____

To do my best writing, I need _____

# Use Multidynamic, Learner-Centered Rubrics

Rubrics are wonderful tools to clarify your expectations for quality products and performances. Rubrics include a scale of value about the standards of excellence expected. The range of quality may be described in as few as three levels or as many as five or even more. A multidynamic rubric will include several traits or categories that will be assessed. Rubrics designed for student use should be clear, concise, and easy to interpret. Some rubrics can be generic and others may be designed for a specific product or performance. "The most effective rubrics help students explore *qualitative* differences in their work, rather than *quantitative* differences" (Tomlinson and Eidson 2003a, 185).

Common elements to include in a rubric:

- Determine the *outcomes* and *objectives* of the task.
- Identify a set of *criteria* that is to be fulfilled.
- Develop *traits* that will serve as the basis for assessment.
- Create *definitions* and *examples* to clarify the traits.
- Determine a *scale of value* on which to rate each trait (such as descriptors or numbers).
- Visualize and include examples of *standards of excellence* for performance levels. (Ask yourself, "What would a good one look like?")

Well-designed rubrics can be used for

- ongoing feedback and formative assessment during the learning
- self-assessment by the student
- summative evaluation and grading
- goal setting

If at all possible, students should know the rubric criteria, traits, and the scale of value to be used when they are given the task or assignment. Reviewing the categories, standards of excellence, and traits that will be used for assessment, and possibly evaluation, leaves little ambiguity about the expectations for successful completion.

As students become familiar with using rubrics, they should be able to include them in the design of the assessment and evaluation criteria for many tasks and assignments. When my third- and fourth-grade students were completing their minireports on an everyday thing, they developed the rubric on page 161. They used the rubric to establish what the expectations were, then for self-assessment, and eventually for peer assessments. I used their rubric as part of the final evaluation. Before the project was to be completed, I sent the rubric home to parents. They *loved* it! Many commented on how the rubric made it easier to coach and support their children to do the work at home.

> Teachers use assessment to gather information to determine what next steps are necessary to ensure students meet the standards and objectives. . . . Assessment often happens informally throughout instruction. . . . When the students' work is graded and the grades cannot change, the students' work has been evaluated—not assessed. . . . Evaluations are judgments that fall at the end of learning, and for many result in discouragement and withdrawal.
>
> —Spencer Rogers and the Peak Learning Team (2003, 44–45)

David Lazear, author of *The Rubrics Way: Using MI to Assess Understanding* (1990) and many other books on the multiple intelligences, believes that, "Many of the authenticity difficulties we face today come from the divorce between instruction and assessment. They must be wed again if we are to assess students in authentic ways that genuinely serve the ultimate goals of promoting deep understanding" (13). If students don't know when they are being assessed, they won't worry about it. Frequent, ongoing assessment should guide instructional planning based on the data collected. By providing immediate feedback to students, you can avoid having them "lose it or confuse it." For students, learning techniques for self-assessment is an important life skill and should become an integral part of the learning process.

# Multidynamic Project Assessment Rubric

|  | Awesome<br>4 | A Good Effort<br>3 | A Work in Progress<br>2 | Just Beginning<br>1 |
|---|---|---|---|---|
| **Organization** | • Extremely well organized<br>• Easy to follow<br>• Flows smoothly | • Some organization<br>• Most ideas flowed<br>• Thoughtful arrangement | • Somewhat disorganized<br>• Ideas didn't flow<br>• Some confusion | • Incoherent<br>• Difficult to follow<br>• Lacked format |
| **Content Accuracy and Understanding** | • Comprehensive and accurate facts<br>• Detailed explanations add to reader's understanding | • Most facts accurate<br>• Some explanations weren't clearly developed | • Somewhat accurate<br>• Inconsistent explanations | • Based on assumed information; misleading<br>• Facts not accurate or documented |
| **Comprehensive Research** | • Went above and beyond to gather research<br>• Used six or more resources | • Used a variety of resources<br>• Used four or more resources | • Used limited resources provided in class<br>• No evidence of consulting outside resources | • Ineffective use of resources<br>• Did little or no research<br>• No documentation |
| **Presentation and Mechanics** | • Ideas presented in an organized and original manner<br>• Impeccable mechanics | • Ideas presented in an effective manner<br>• Few mechanical errors | • Inconsistent presentation of ideas<br>• Many mechanical errors—draft format | • Lacked effective presentation qualities<br>• Ideas unclear<br>• First-draft quality |
| **Novelty and Creativity** | • Cleverly and uniquely arranged<br>• Original ideas, artwork, and graphics enhanced total project | • Thoughtfully presented<br>• Additional artwork and illustrations added interest | • Few original touches to enhance project<br>• Some basic clipart<br>• Little time spent developing | • Predictable<br>• Just covered basics<br>• No added artwork or other elements to add interest |
| **Technology Integration** | • Project included PowerPoint slides, video, Internet links, or web site<br>• Used technology extensively for research and presentation | • Project included technology use<br>• Used technology sources for some research | • Little evidence of technology use<br>• Research limited to print | • Lacking any use of technology for research, presentation, or creation |

Adapted from *Begin with the Brain*, by Martha Kaufeldt, © 1999 Zephyr Press. Used with permission.

# "Everyday Thing" Minireport Rubric

| **Super Effort +** <br> What a great report <br> would look like: | **Medium Effort √** <br> What an OK report <br> would look like: | **Beginning Effort –** <br> What a report that needs <br> more work would look like: |
| --- | --- | --- |
| • *Great* handwriting <br><br> • Interesting details <br><br> • Proper grammar— good sentences and paragraphs <br><br> • Appropriate punctuation <br><br> • Spelling checked and corrected <br><br> • Several good illustrations: color, big, details, appropriate <br><br> • Correct capitalization <br><br> • Good word choices <br><br> • Neatly arranged <br><br> • Colorful cover <br><br> • Catchy title <br><br> • Meets length requirements | • Handwriting is sometimes messy <br><br> • A few details <br><br> • Some good sentences and paragraphs <br><br> • Some punctuation errors <br><br> • Some spelling errors <br><br> • A few illustrations, no color, messy <br><br> • Some capitalization errors <br><br> • Some inappropriate words <br><br> • Not put together with care—a little messy <br><br> • Plain cover <br><br> • Average title <br><br> • Too long or too short | • Messy handwriting <br><br> • No details and boring information <br><br> • Poor sentences and paragraphs <br><br> • Many punctuation errors <br><br> • Many spelling errors <br><br> • No illustrations <br><br> • Capitalization not checked <br><br> • Inappropriate words <br><br> • Unfinished or very messy <br><br> • Boring or no cover <br><br> • Boring or inappropriate title, or no title <br><br> • Too short |

## *Tackle Box Ideas*

♦ Develop at least one assessment strategy to use as immediate feedback to students as well as to gather information to guide instruction.

♦ Orchestrate a KWL activity or a Readiness Checklist *before* beginning a new lesson (see the examples on pages 147 and 148).

♦ Create a simple three-point rubric to assess student progress as they *build* understanding (see page 161).

# 11
# Starting with Baby Steps

*What You Can Do Today*

▶ Prepare students and parents for differentiated instruction.

▶ Distinguish between and prioritize low-preparation and high-preparation strategies.

▶ Build your tackle box of instructional strategies with colleagues and through professional growth.

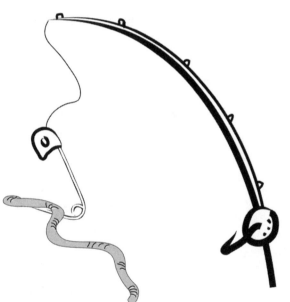

*A*lways bear in mind that your own resolution to succeed is more important than any other one thing.

—*Abraham Lincoln*

When my family and I have an opportunity to teach others how to fish, we start with simple strategies, equipment, and expectations. More than once we have outfitted a beginner with a simple pole (no reel!), a modest length of line, a barbless hook, and a single salmon egg for bait. If the new anglers aren't having much luck, we graduate them to a different bait, or location on the dock, and eventually to a fully rigged rod and reel. As we help them understand the fish habits and fishing techniques, they usually begin to experiment with new techniques themselves.

As you expand your own repertoire of teaching strategies to differentiate instruction, allow yourself to begin with baby steps. As teachers, we experience enough stress as it is. Please don't let this seem so daunting that you go into a reflexive response yourself. Here are a few suggestions as you start your journey.

## Prepare Students and Parents for Differentiated Instruction

Integrating differentiated instruction into daily lessons and activities takes some practice. Some teachers already vary instructional strategies on a regular basis. They have developed systems to allow choice, and students know that learning takes place in different ways in that classroom. As you prepare your students for differentiated instruction (as outlined on page 139), keep in mind the need to prepare parents as well.

Send home a letter to parents and make a presentation at Back to School Night about your intentions for differentiated instruction. To some parents, the different instructional strategies that you will be using might "look different" than previous techniques. Parents of teenagers sometimes comment that the activities, at first glance, look more elementary than traditional secondary assignments. When they see the incredible learning going on, the complexity of the tasks, and the success of the students, however, they are usually convinced of the new techniques' effectiveness.

The issue of fairness will come up for parents also. Parents of struggling students as well as of capable learners are wary that different activities might give some students an unfair advantage or that the task may be "too easy" for their child. The question of "How will you grade these fairly?" may come up, so have an answer ready! Reassure parents that the groupings, tasks, and strategies are all flexible and that you will adapt assignments as necessary.

Include parent input in creating a student profile. Parents can be valuable resources for determining a student's learning preferences, MI strengths, work habits, and prior successes or challenges at school. Write letters to parents (see the example on page 166), design a questionnaire for parents to fill out and return (see page 167), and arrange conferences with as many parents as possible.

Send home clear assignment information sheets and, if possible, the rubric for assessment. Parents are usually very happy to support the instructional strategies if they know what the expectations are (that is, "What would a 'good one' look like?").

## Distinguish Between and Prioritize Low-Preparation and High-Preparation Strategies

Start where you are. Examine how well you are already

- honoring individual students' unique learning styles (see page 27)
- teaching with the multiple intelligences in mind (see page 101)
- offering options for how students demonstrate their understanding (choice; see page 102)
- grouping students with various partners and in small, interactive, flexible groups (see pages 46–49)
- introducing new information in diverse ways, including using the discovery process (see pages 58–60)
- providing feedback and assessment on a regular basis (see page 144)

# Chapter 11

# Parent Letter Example

March 17, 2003

Dear parents of third- and fourth-graders at Tierra Pacifica,

I am very excited to be returning to the classroom this week! I was a classroom teacher for over 23 years in the SLV and Santa Cruz Districts. As many of you know, my most recent job was as the lead teacher in the intermediate class at Monarch Community School from 1992 to 1997. I wrote a book on brain-compatible learning strategies and have been working as a teacher trainer and keynote speaker all over North America. I love working with adults and feel I have made an impact on thousands of students, but I miss teaching kids. I am looking forward to this opportunity, and I am eager to get to know your children.

I am committed and confident that together we can create a low-stress transition as J. leaves the class to begin her life as a new mom. I will meet several more times with her this week to understand the schedule, curriculum, and strategies that she has been implementing. Then, as it seems appropriate, we may make some modifications to things. I have a lot of ideas, strategies, and units that I think would be beneficial and fun that we may want to work in before the end of the year.

Although many of you were at the meeting last Monday when I introduced myself, I didn't get to be introduced to each of you at all! I am attaching a Meet the Parents questionnaire to this letter. If you could take a moment to respond to some of the queries and return it to school ASAP, then I will have a better understanding of what your expectations are for your child at school. We have a tentative evening meeting planned for April 7th, where I can share some suggestions and we can discuss priorities for the rest of the year and get to know each other a little better. I will also be available for individual conferences as needed.

I have also included a list of Life Skills for Success, which is from my book. I have integrated and developed these skills into varied lessons that involve group activities, community building, journal writing, and literature selections. On the Meet the Parents questionnaire, you can let me know which ones you think we should focus on in the next few weeks.

Today I gave the students a little booklet that I would like them to fill out over the next few days to help me get to know them more quickly. They can respond in writing or draw pictures. At the parent meeting I will give you a copy of a short survey that I would like to give the students to help you and I better understand which of the multiple intelligences are their strengths and which ones they have yet to develop. (There is no scoring involved or numbers and labels.)

The main focus of a brain-compatible classroom is to be an emotionally and physically safe and secure learning environment as well as maintaining challenge for each student. As I begin teaching in the third- and fourth-grade classroom at Tierra Pacifica, that is my commitment to you and your children. If there is something of concern to you, don't hesitate to call me (462-XXXX).

I look forward to working with you and your child.

Martha Kaufeldt

# Meet the Parents

Student's name: _____

Parent(s) name(s): _____

Teacher: _____ Grade: _____ Date: _____

Please take a few minutes to respond briefly to the following questions. All responses are confidential. This is an efficient way to help me to get to know a little about you and your child. I look forward to meeting you in person soon!

★ ★ ★ ★ ★ ★ ★ ★ ★ ★ ★ ★ ★ ★ ★ ★ ★ ★ ★ ★ ★ ★ ★ ★ ★

What are the main reasons why you have your child at this school?

What is your family's configuration? Does your child share living time with another parent?

Describe your employment or time outside the home. What hours are you gone?

Does your child go to before- or afterschool care?

On average, about how many hours a day does your child spend on technology-dependent activities (such as TV, computer, video games, telephone, etc.)?

What organized extracurricular activities does your child participate in?

What subjects in school seem to be your child's most challenging?

In what subjects in school is your child most successful?

In general, how do you and your child feel about his or her school experience last year?

What are your expectations about assigned homework from school?

What subjects or skills do you hope I emphasize in the next year?

Are there any special circumstances or events in your child's life that you think I should know about right now (such as divorce, illness, moving, income, etc.)?

What else do you want me to know in order to get to know you or your child better? Do you have any concerns?

♦ designing a wide range of challenging, complex tasks (see pages 119–29)

♦ modifying and accommodating assignments for struggling students and ESL learners (see pages 140–41)

A great way to begin is to expand an activity or task that you have already been using. If students have already been researching and writing, then consider extending the assignment to include a choice activity. After students wrote minireports on an "everyday thing," I had them select from the choices listed below. The inquiries were limited—too many can overwhelm us and the students! The tasks also represented several of the multiple intelligences. All students were able to find and select something that worked for them.

---

**EVERYDAY THING PROJECT AND PRESENTATION**

Now that you have finished your written report on an "everyday thing," you need to present your information to the class. Use your knowledge, creativity, and your most developed "smarts" (multiple intelligences) to create a project or make a presentation. Do your *personal best.* Make sure the information you share includes at least five key points that you think we should remember.

**Choose** at least *one* of the following projects to complete by May 2nd. Hugger Muggers choose two!

- **Create** a colorful 3-D triorama. Show your everyday thing being used in a scene from any time period. Use labels to show at least five key points.
- **Perform** a skit for the class: Either create and perform a commercial for the everyday thing or pretend that you are the inventor sharing your new ideas at a convention. Include at least five key points.
- **Create** a colorful timeline of the history of your everyday thing. Include at least six dates. Use some drawings or icons and symbols.
- **Compose** a song (such as a rap) about your everyday thing. Include at least five key points and facts in the song. Be prepared to perform it for the class. Wear a costume or use a prop when you share it. Write down the words and turn them in.

---

## 10 Low-Prep Strategies

1. Encourage students to use highlighting pens and Post-it notes on worksheets, readings, and research assignments.

2. Teach basic Mind Mapping (webbing) strategies for note taking, prewriting, and agendas. *Mapping Inner Space*, by Nancy Margulies with Nusa Maal (2002), is a terrific resource. Encourage the use of simple graphics.

3. Organize the class so that each student is assigned to at least one small group and two partner pairings. Use these groupings often for discussions, projects, processing, and collaborative tasks (see pages 46–49).

4. Limit direct instruction and "teacher talk time" to only 15 minutes per instructional hour or class period.

5. Try to offer at least one choice activity per week (see pages 102–107). Limit choices to just two or three activities.

6. Display a daily class agenda to help students see the game plan for the day.

7. Try a jigsaw activity (see pages 69–72) and have each group research or read an aspect of the lesson and report to the rest of the class.

8. Ask for an exit card as each student's "ticket out the door" after a lesson (see page 155).

9. Have students share a "thumbs ups" or "thumbs down" (agree or disagree) as you read factual and fictional statements.

10. Post four choices, responses, or answers in four corners of the room. Have students stand in the corner that best matches their own opinion or answer.

## 10 High-Prep Strategies

1. Organize students into tribes that serve as their base group for the entire year (see pages 44–46). Orchestrate inclusion activities to build a sense of belonging in the tribes.

2. Design a series of lessons that help students understand the multiple intelligences (see page 20). Have students complete a survey about their own strengths (see pages 23–25). Organize tasks and activities with MI in mind (see page 101).

3. Create a work area in the classroom that allows kinesthetic learners to stand up and move around. Encourage these students to use this area often.

4. Develop a system for homework that allows students to have some "must do's" and some "may do's" (see page 104). Make sure that the choice options are meaningful, relevant, and use various intelligences.

5. Create checklists and simple rubrics that you and the students can use for feedback as they *build* their understanding (see pages 155 and 158–61).

6. Teach students about Bloom's taxonomy and higher-level thinking (see page 127). Encourage them to submit good proposals for activities and tasks.

7. Organize a meaningful evening learning celebration as a culminating project so that students can demonstrate their new understandings to family and the community.

8. Work with colleagues and the school administrators to create longer periods of *uninterrupted protected time.* Be a strong advocate for a flexible schedule that allows students to get into flow (see page 73).

9. Design an integrated thematic unit of study for your own class or with another teacher (see page 68).

10. Promote use of technology to build and demonstrate student understanding. Integrate PowerPoint presentations, digital cameras, music, the Internet, and video production in your own lessons.

## Build Your Tackle Box with Colleagues and through Professional Growth

By reading this book, you've already begun to take steps toward building up your tackle box. Teaching can be a very isolating endeavor. Just as I believe that students can learn from each other if we encourage collaboration, I believe that teachers must make a commitment to share strategies and ideas with colleagues. If we want no child left behind, we must work cooperatively. Teaching shouldn't be about whose students have the highest test scores—it is not a competition! By reaching out to our own "teachers down the hall," we ensure that no *teacher* shall be left behind.

There are many incredible books, videos, and websites available to teachers. I hope you are inspired to continue building your tackle box with multiple strategies, from various sources. As you discover something that works for you, be sure to offer the idea to a teacher friend. Encourage others to share as well. Begin a Tackle Box bulletin board in the staff room at your school.

Keep on the lookout for professional development opportunities that build your understanding and application of the following topics:

- ◆ multiple intelligences
- ◆ learning styles
- ◆ strategies for ADD and ADHD students
- ◆ cooperative learning and flexible grouping
- ◆ extension activities for gifted and capable learners
- ◆ modifications and adaptations for struggling learners
- ◆ strategies for ESL learners
- ◆ integrating visual and performing arts
- ◆ Mind Mapping and graphic organizers
- ◆ movement and games for kinesthetic learners
- ◆ presentation and direct instruction techniques

- integrating technology into lessons and student projects
- discovery process and project-based learning
- authentic assessment and rubrics

A good angler is dedicated, persistent, patient, clever, and always on the lookout for a new technique, lure, or strategy. Good luck as you learn to change your bait to meet the needs of your unique students.

# Bibliography

Anderson, Lorin W., and David Krathwohl, eds. 2001. *A Taxonomy for Learning, Teaching, and Assessing: A Revision of Bloom's Taxonomy of Educational Objectives.* New York: Longman.

Armstrong, Thomas. 2000. *Multiple Intelligences in the Classroom.* 2nd ed. Alexandria, Va.: Association for Supervision and Curriculum Development.

———. 2003. *You're Smarter Than You Think: A Kid's Guide to Multiple Intelligences.* Minneapolis, Minn.: Free Spirit Publishing.

ASCD [Association for Supervision and Curriculum Development]. 2005. *A Lexicon of Learning: What Educators Mean When They Say . . .* Alexandria, Va.: ASCD. http://www.ascd.org/cms/index.cfm?TheViewID=1123 (accessed January 30, 2005).

Belvel, Patricia Sequeira, and Maya Marcia Jordan. 2003. *Rethinking Classroom Management: Strategies for Prevention, Intervention, and Problem Solving.* Thousand Oaks, Calif.: Corwin Press.

Benjamin, Amy. 2003. *Differentiated Instruction: A Guide for Elementary School Teachers.* Larchmont, N.Y.: Eye On Education.

Bloom, Benjamin S., ed. 1956. *Taxonomy of Educational Objectives: The Classification of Educational Goals by a Committee of College and University Examiners.* New York: Longmans, Green.

Bransford, John D., Ann L. Brown, and Rodney R. Cocking, eds. 1999. *How People Learn: Brain, Mind, Experience, and School.* Committee on Developments in the Science of Learning, Commission on Behavioral and Social Sciences and Education, National Research Council. Washington, D.C.: National Academy Press.

Brooks, Jacqueline, and Martin Brooks. 1993. *In Search of Understanding: The Case for Constructivist Classrooms.* Alexandria, Va.: ASCD.

Caine, Renate Nummela, and Geoffrey Caine. 1994. *Making Connections: Teaching and the Human Brain.* Menlo Park, Calif.: Addison-Wesley.

———. 1999. *Mindshifts.* Tucson, Ariz.: Zephyr Press.

Cohen, Elizabeth. 1994. *Designing Groupwork: Strategies for the Heterogeneous Classroom.* 2nd ed. New York: Teachers College Press.

Csikszentmihalyi, Mihaly. 1990. *Flow: The Psychology of Optimal Experience.* New York: Harper and Row.

Davies, Anne. 2000. *Making Classroom Assessment Work.* Courtenay, B.C.: Connections Publishing.

Diamond, Marian, and Janet Hopson. 1998. *Magic Trees of the Mind: How to Nurture Your Child's Intelligence, Creativity, and Healthy Emotions from Birth through Adolescence.* New York: Dutton.

Donovan, M. Suzanne, John D. Bransford, and James W. Pellegrino, eds. 1999. *How People Learn: Bridging Research and Practice.* Prepared for the Committee on Learning Research and Educational Practice, Commission on Behavioral and Social Sciences and Education, National Research Council. Washington, D.C. : National Academy Press.

Ellis, Arthur K. 2001. *Research on Educational Innovations.* 3rd ed. Larchmont, N.Y.: Eye On Education.

Erickson, H. Lynn. 2001. *Stirring the Head, Heart, and Soul: Redefining Curriculum and Instruction.* 2nd ed. Thousand Oaks, Calif.: Corwin Press.

Erlauer, Laura. 2003. *The Brain-Compatible Classroom: Using What We Know About Learning to Improve Teaching.* Alexandria, Va.: ASCD.

Forsten, Char, Jim Grant, and Betty Hollas. 2002. *Differentiated Instruction: Different Strategies for Different Learners.* Peterborough, N.H.: Crystal Springs Books.

Gardner, Howard. 1993. *Multiple Intelligences: The Theory in Practice.* New York: Basic Books.

Gibbs, Jeanne. 1995. *Tribes: A New Way of Learning and Being Together.* Santa Rosa, Calif.: Center Source Publications.

———. 2001. *Discovering Gifts in Middle School: Learning in a Caring Culture Called Tribes.* Windsor, Calif.: CenterSource Systems.

Goleman, Daniel. 1995. *Emotional Intelligence.* New York: Bantam.

Gopnik, Alison, Andrew N. Meltzoff, and Patricia Kuhl. 1999. *The Scientist in the Crib: Minds, Brains and How Children Learn.* New York: William Morrow and Company.

Gregory, Gayle H., and Carolyn Chapman. 2002. *Differentiated Instructional Strategies: One Size Doesn't Fit All.* Thousand Oaks, Calif.: Corwin Press.

Hammond, Linda Darling. 1997. *The Right to Learn: A Blueprint for Creating Schools That Work.* San Francisco: Jossey-Bass.

Hart, Leslie A. 1999. *Human Brain and Human Learning.* Covington, Wash.: Books for Educators.

Hathaway, W. E., J. A. Hargreaves, G. W. Thompson, and D. Novitsky. 1992. *A Study into the Effects of Light on Children of Elementary School Age—A Case of Daylight Robbery.* Report prepared for the Department of Education, Edmonton, Alberta.

Heacox, Diane. 2002. *Differentiating Instruction in the Regular Classroom: How to Reach and Teach All Learners, Grades 3–12.* Minneapolis, Minn.: Free Spirit.

Healy, Jane. 1994. *Your Child's Growing Mind: A Guide to Learning and Brain Development from Birth to Adolescence.* Rev. ed. New York: Doubleday.

———. 1999. *Endangered Minds: Why Children Don't Think—And What We Can Do About It.* New York: Simon and Schuster.

Jensen, Eric. 1997. *Brain-Compatible Strategies.* San Diego, Calif.: Brain Store.

———. 2000. *Different Brains, Different Learners: How to Reach the Hard to Reach.* San Diego, Calif.: Brain Store.

———. 2003a. *A New View of AD/HD: Success Strategies for the Impulsive Learner.* San Diego, Calif.: Brain Store.

———. 2003b. *Tools for Engagement: Managing Emotional States for Learner Success.* San Diego, Calif.: Brain Store.

Jensen, Eric, with Michael Dabney. 2000. *Learning Smarter: The New Science of Teaching.* San Diego, Calif.: Brain Store.

———. 2003. *Environments for Learning.* San Diego, Calif.: Brain Store.

Kagan, Spencer. 1992. *Silly Sports and Goofy Games.* San Clemente, Calif.: Resources for Teachers.

———. 1994. *Cooperative Learning.* San Clemente, Calif.: Resources for Teachers.

Kaufeldt, Martha. 1999. *Begin with the Brain: Orchestrating the Learner-Centered Classroom.* Tucson, Ariz.: Zephyr Press.

Kotulak, Ronald. 1997. *Inside the Brain.* Kansas City, Mo.: Andrews McMeel Publishing.

Lazear, David G. 1990. *The Rubrics Way: Using MI to Assess Understanding.* Tucson, Ariz.: Zephyr Press.

———. 2000. *The Intelligent Curriculum: Using Multiple Intelligences to Develop Your Students' Full Potential.* Tucson, Ariz.: Zephyr Press.

Le Doux, Joseph. 1996. *The Emotional Brain: The Mysterious Underpinnings of Emotional Life.* New York: Touchstone.

Margulies, Nancy, with Nusa Maal. 2002. *Mapping Inner Space.* Revised ed. Tucson, Ariz.: Zephyr Press.

Margulies, Nancy, and Christine Valenza. 2005. *Visual Thinking: Tools for Mapping Your Ideas.* Norwalk, Conn.: Crown House Publishing.

Marzano, Robert J., Debra J. Pickering, and Jane E. Pollock. 2001. *Classroom Instruction That Works: Research-Based Strategies for Increasing Student Achievement.* Alexandria, Va.: ASCD.

Murdock, George. 1945. "The Common Denominator of Cultures." In *The Science of Man in the World Crisis,* ed. Ralph Linton, 123–42. New York: Columbia University Press.

Newmann, Fred M. 1991. "Linking Restructuring to Authentic Student Achievement." *Phi Delta Kappan* (72) 6: 458–63.

———. 1996. *Authentic Achievement: Restructuring Schools for Intellectual Quality.* San Francisco: Jossey-Bass Publishers.

Newmann, Fred M., and Gary G. Wehlage. 1993. "Five Standards of Authentic Instruction." *Educational Leadership* (50) 7: 8–12.

Perkins, David. 1995. *Outsmarting IQ: The Emerging Science of Learnable Intelligence.* New York: Simon and Schuster.

Reis, Sally M., and Joseph S. Renzulli. 2004. "Curriculum Compacting: A Systematic Procedure for Modifying the Curriculum for Above Average Ability Students." Storrs: National Research Center on the Gifted and Talented, University of Connecticut. http://www.sp.uconn.edu/~nrcgt/sem/semart08.html (accessed September 16, 2004).

Rogers, Spencer, with the Peak Learning Team. 2003. *21 Building Blocks Critical to Leaving No Child Behind.* Evergreen, Colo.: Peak Learning Systems.

Sapolsky, Robert. 1998. *Why Zebras Don't Get Ulcers: An Updated Guide to Stress, Stress-Related Disease and Coping.* New York: W.H. Freeman and Company.

Schwartz, Ellen. 1999. "What to Give Your Kids? Time, Affection, and Optimism." Interview with Barbara Coloroso in *Costco Connections* 12, no. 4 (July/August): 33–34.

Siegel, Daniel J. 1999. *The Developing Mind: Toward a Neurobiology of Interpersonal Experience.* New York: Guilford Press.

Silver, Harvey F., Richard W. Strong, and Matthew J. Perini. 2000. *So Each May Learn: Integrating Learning Styles and Multiple Intelligences.* Alexandria, Va.: ASCD.

Smith, Alistair. 2005. *The Brain's Behind It: New Knowledge about the Brain and Learning.* Norwalk, Conn.: Crown House Publishing.

Smith, Frank. 1986. *Insult to Intelligence: The Bureaucratic Invasion of Our Classrooms.* New York: Arbor House.

Sneider, Cary I., and Katharine Barrett, with Kevin Beals, Lincoln Bergman, Jefferey S. Kaufmann, and Robert C. Knott. 1999. *River Cutters.* Berkeley, Calif.: GEMS, Lawrence Hall of Science, University of California.

Society for Neuroscience. 2002. *Brain Facts: A Primer on the Brain and Nervous System.* 4th ed. Washington, D.C.: Society for Neuroscience.

Sousa, David A. 2001. *How the Brain Learns: A Classroom Teacher's Guide.* 2nd ed. Thousand Oaks, Calif.: Corwin Press.

Sprenger, Marilee. 2002. *Becoming a "Wiz" at Brain-Based Teaching: How to Make Every Year Your Best Year.* Thousand Oaks, Calif.: Corwin Press.

Sternberg, Robert J., ed. 2000. *Handbook of Intelligence.* New York: Cambridge University Press.

Sylwester, Robert. 1995. *A Celebration of Neurons: An Educator's Guide to the Human Brain.* Alexandria, Va.: ASCD.

———. 2000. *A Biological Brain in a Cultural Classroom.* Thousand Oaks, Calif.: Corwin Press.

———. 2005. *How to Explain a Brain: An Educator's Handbook of Brain Terms and Cognitive Processes.* Thousand Oaks, Calif.: Corwin Press.

Tomlinson, Carol Ann. 1999. *The Differentiated Classroom: Responding to the Needs of All Learners.* Alexandria, Va.: ASCD.

———. 2001. *How to Differentiate Instruction in Mixed-Ability Classrooms.* 2nd ed. Alexandria, Va.: ASCD.

Tomlinson, Carol Ann, and Caroline Cunningham Eidson. 2003a. *Differentiation in Practice: A Resource Guide for Differentiating Curriculum, Grades K–5.* Alexandria, Va.: ASCD.

———. 2003b. *Differentiation in Practice: A Resource Guide for Differentiating Curriculum, Grades 5–9.* Alexandria, Va.: ASCD.

Walker Tileston, Donna. 2004. *What Every Teacher Should Know About Effective Teaching Strategies.* Thousand Oaks, Calif.: Corwin Press.

Wiggins, Grant, and Jay McTighe. 1998. *Understanding by Design.* Alexandria, Va.: ASCD.

Wolfe, Patricia. 2001. *Brain Matters: Translating Research into Classroom Practice.* Alexandria, Va.: ASCD.

Wolfe, Patricia, and Pamela Nevills. 2004. *Building the Reading Brain* (Pre-K–3). Thousand Oaks, Calif.: Corwin Press.

Zull, James. 2002. *The Art of Changing the Brain.* Sterling, Va.: Stylus Publishing.

## Internet Resources

Useful websites are listed throughout the book. Here are a few more that are well worth your time to explore.

- ▶ Dana Alliance for Brain Initiatives: http://www.dana.org

- ▶ Brain Connection: http://www.brainconnection.com

- ▶ New Horizons for Learning: http://www.newhorizons.org

- ▶ The Krasnow Institute for Advanced Study at George Mason University: http://www.gmu.edu/departments/krasnow

# Index

**Note:** Page numbers in **bold** indicate information that may be useful for a handout